Historic Tales of
Jamestown

Historic Tales of
Jamestown

Rosemary Enright
& Sue Maden

The History Press

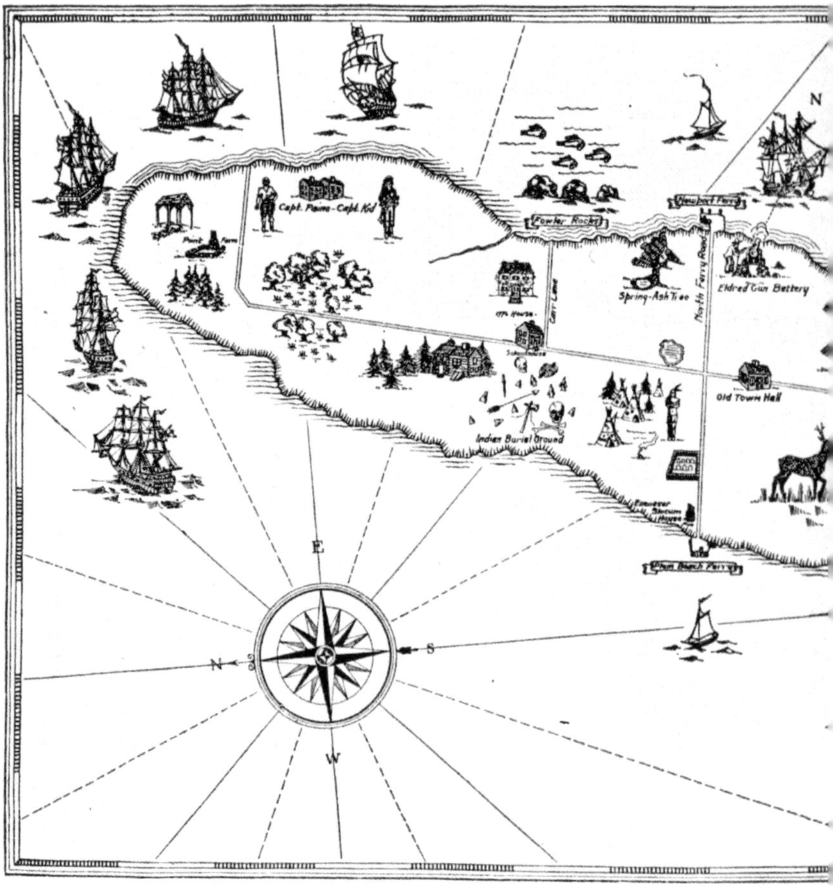

A map of Jamestown celebrating the important sites and activities of the seventeenth and eighteenth centuries. *Jamestown Historical Society (A2006.409.008).*

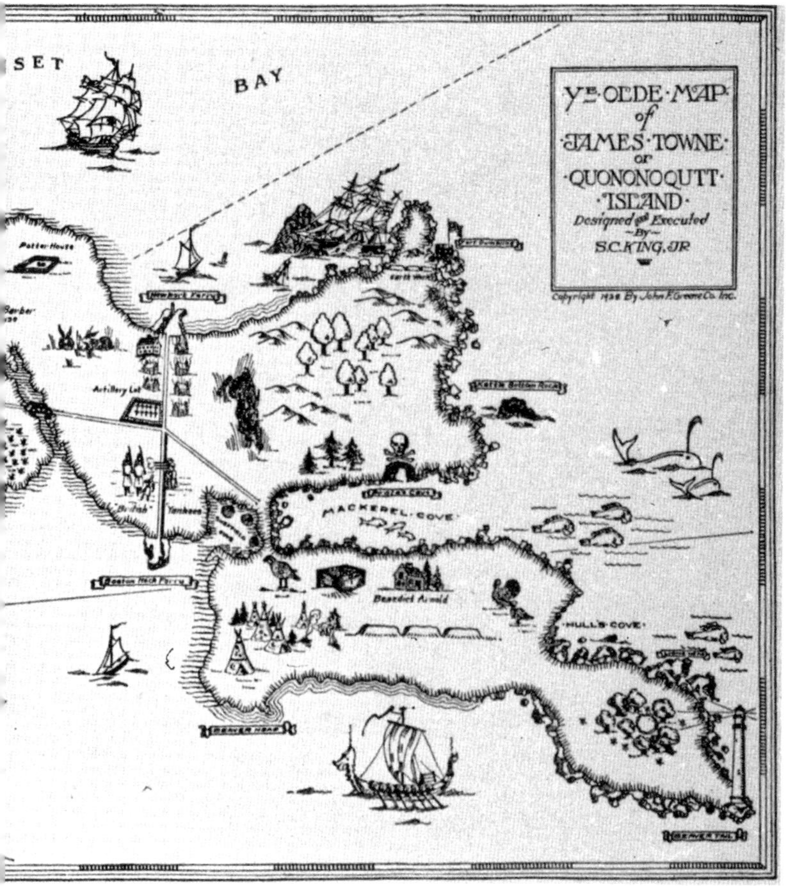

Ye Olde Map of James Towne or Quononoqutt Island
Designed and Executed By S.C. King, Jr.
SET
BAY
Potter House
Artillery Lot
Yankees
Boston Neck Ferry
Kettle Bottom Rock
MACKEREL · COVE
Benedict Arnold
HULL'S COVE

Published by The History Press
Charleston, SC
www.historypress.net

Back cover: Jamestown Historical Society collection.

First published 2016

Manufactured in the United States

ISBN 978.1.62619.955.2

Library of Congress Control Number: 2015955759

Contents

Preface

Historic Tales of Jamestown grew out of a series of articles that Sue and I wrote for the *Jamestown Press* about the history of Jamestown.

Neither Sue nor I is a native Jamestowner. Sue's roots are deeper than mine—her great-grandmother built a summer home overlooking the West Passage of Narragansett Bay in 1896. Sue was brought to Jamestown before her first birthday, spent many youthful summers here, and moved here permanently in 1982. I married a summer Jamestowner whose family had been coming to the island since the 1880s. My husband and I settled here year-round in 1974.

Perhaps it is our status as outsiders who have had to learn the history of our community, rather than natives who have grown up as part of it, that gave birth to our fascination with the subject.

Sue has been researching and co-authoring articles and books about Jamestown for over twenty-five years—West Ferry Press published her first Jamestown book, *Greetings from Jamestown, Rhode Island: Picture Post Card Views 1900–1950,* in 1988, and her first articles appeared in the *Jamestown Press* in 1992. Many of the articles she wrote with Patrick Hodgkin in the early 1990s were published in *Jamestown Affairs: A Miscellany of Historical Flashbacks* in 1996.

I joined the list of her co-authors in 2009 when we wrote a monograph for the Jamestown Historical Society about keepers of the Dutch Island light. Since then we have written two books and more than fifty articles about the history of Jamestown.

Our work pattern for our articles is well established. Sue identifies people, events, places, or eras that she finds interesting and thinks will interest others. Together, we decide which ones to tackle in detail. Sue does the research, combing through town records, historical society documents, newspapers, taped interviews, census data—any resource she can find. If the event is recent enough—often it isn't—she talks to the people involved.

I take her detailed research and weave the facts into a story. Sometimes the story I put together needs some corroborating information. Sue finds it. If she can't, or if the new facts she discovers change the meaning or importance of other events, I rewrite until we are both happy. We then hand it off to Harry Wright, our arbiter for grammar, organization, and common sense.

We followed the same pattern for this book, with the notable exception that half of the articles were based on our own essays for the *Jamestown Press*.

ROSEMARY ENRIGHT
November 2015

Acknowledgements

We are very grateful to all the people who have helped us with this effort.

Harry Wright read and reread these essays, and without him, they would not read as smoothly.

Jeff McDonough, publisher of the *Jamestown Press*, gave us room in his newspaper for the original articles and permission to use them here. The bibliography contains a list of the articles we incorporated or referenced. Almost all of them were rewritten—sometimes to change the slant of the story, sometimes to put the essay in context, sometimes to lengthen or shorten the original. And sometimes just because.

The Jamestown Historical Society gave us unlimited access to its archives and permission to use photographs and graphics from the collection. We especially thank the Collections Committee, of which we are both members, for helping us find material we needed and for ignoring our frequent lack of attention to the business of the society.

Many people—too numerous to mention—contributed to the original articles that were the genesis of this book. Joe Bains, Emeline Cabral, Archie Clarke, members of the Daggett family, Elizabeth Di Censo, Mary Greene, Judy Hannold, Carol Hopkins, and Ryan Weeden were the sources for stories and pictures that are new for this collection.

The personnel in the town clerk's office were always helpful, particularly in our use of land evidence, vital records, and official minutes of the town council and financial town meetings.

Ken Carlson, reference archivist at the Rhode Island State Archives; the reference department at the Seattle Public Library; and the staff of our own Jamestown Philomenian Library answered numerous questions.

And finally, we thank our readers Joyce Allphin, Ralph Klingbeil, Lois Migneault, and Ginny Saunders for pointing out errors or infelicities that escaped Harry's eagle eyes.

Part I
Early Days

Chapter 1

Beginnings

Although the history of Conanicut Island begins in the distant past, the first document that is uniquely Jamestown's is the 1657 Land Agreement. This document, to which all land claims on Conanicut and Dutch Islands are traced, is a pre-purchase agreement among buyers about land they expect to buy. Gould Island, which is also a part of Jamestown, was purchased the same year but was not part of the 1657 agreement.

In the document, a brief preamble is followed by twelve numbered articles. The preamble states the reasons for wanting to purchase "Quononaqutt" (now Conanicut) Island.

> *First forasmuch, as it is frequently declared that of late there have been endeavors used by some who are neither inhabitants of this Island nor members of this Colony, to get into their possession and power of disposal the abovesaid Island quononaqutt, And—*
>
> *Secondly considering how Commodiously the said Island lies for the enlarging the accommodations of some of us, in regard of the nearness of it to our dwellings, As also considering the great straight that many of us are in for want of commonage for Cattle, as also for other occasions therefore*
>
> *And for the preventing any foreigners getting it into their possession. whereby inconvenience and disturbance, might possibly, yea, and probably, arise to the Government of this Colony.*

After that brief introduction, the men who intended to purchase the land in the middle of the entrance to Narragansett Bay got right down to business. The first article of the contract names seven trustees and authorizes them to negotiate the purchase of the islands from the Narragansett.

> *That for the procuring the aforesaid Island Conanicut for the occasion aforesaid we do hereby Authorize and appoint, seven of our own Number—Namely William Coddington Esq., Benedict Arnold Sr., William Brenton or in his absence William Baulstone in his stead, also Richard Smith Sr., or in his absence his Son Richard Smith of Narragansett, also Captn John Cranston, Caleb Carr and John Sanford, to use the best of their endeavors thereby to Make A full and firm purchase of the aforesaid Island quononaqutt.*

The second article names each prospective purchaser, states his commitment, and lists how much land he will receive as a result of his payment. The article contains the names of five men who did not sign the document. Some of those who committed to purchase the island sold their rights to others before the actual purchase was negotiated and the document was signed.

The article is long and boring to read, although its content is critical. It starts with the men contributing the largest amounts:

> *William Coddington of Newport Esq., and Benedict Arnold of Newport Sr. shall each of them pay one twentieth part of the whole charge, And shall Each of them Receive one twentieth part of the premised purchase, And William Brenton Merchant, shall pay one fortieth part and one hundred & Eleventh part of the whole charge, And shall Receive one fortieth part and one hundred and Eleventh part of the premised purchase…*

And so on for each of the 106 men. The last four named—Thomas Cass, Anthony Ravenscraft, Thomas Oliver, and John Fones—each committed to "one nine hundredth part of the whole charge" in return for "one nine hundredth part of the premised purchase."

The third article creates a sixteen-person "perpetual Council or Committee" to oversee the seven trustees who after the purchase will have "full power to Manage all Matters, concerning the premises." The list of the original sixteen contains most of the important names in southern Rhode Island at that time.

The fourth through the seventh articles establish rules for buying and selling the property proposed to be purchased under the agreement. Perhaps the most important rule, established in article seven, prohibits owners from selling their land to anyone outside the current group of purchasers:

> *We agree that it shall not be lawful for the purchasers or Any of them to dispose or Make any Sale of their or any of their proportions of the premised purchase (as mentioned in the second Article) but only to a purchaser or purchasers of the premises, Except the Aforesaid Trustees being orderly Met, or the Major part of them, approve thereof and consent to the sale thereof to anyone which is not a purchaser...*

The eighth and the ninth articles place the original deeds to the islands in the custody of Benedict Arnold and "true copies"—the equivalent of notarized copies today—of "all material writings" in the custody of John Sanford, who was also responsible for giving copies to individual investors.

The tenth article discusses in a very general way how the land will be surveyed and allocated to individuals and to roads. It also directs the trustees "to lay out about Sixty, two-Acre Shares in some convenient place, for the Situation of A Town."

Fencing is covered in article eleven. Fencing must have been a very controversial topic since the discussion encompasses slightly over 10 percent of the total document. All manner of possible problems are touched on.

No one could be compelled to fence in his land. If a fence was built, it had to be "equally made and maintained...But in case any one have a mind to fence his land, he shall not compel" his neighbor to pay, unless he would benefit from the fence. "If any one have helped as aforesaid to set up and Maintain any such partition Lines of fence he is engaged not to Remove or Demolish the same."

If the fence was not on the property line, and thus of potential benefit to both owners, it should be set back from the line "at least two Rod at Every part of the said line within his own land, which two Rod shall then lie perpetual Common, and this to prevent such, as to oppress the adjoining share by setting the fence a little within his own land, that so his Neighbor may have no commodity by his fence."

Finally, the twelfth article designates Dutch Island "for the use of all the purchasers Each of them having a proportional Right in the same according to the proportion, they shall enjoy of Conanicut."

The last paragraph of the document makes a few minor changes, including documenting Joseph Clarke's authority to sign for his brother

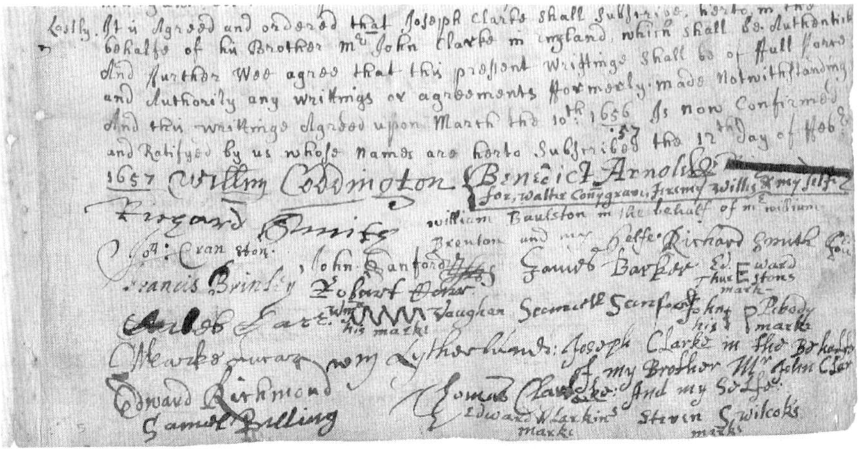
Lastly. It is Agreed and ordered that Joseph Clarke shall Subscribe hereto in the behalfe of his Brother Mr John Clarke in England, which shall be Authentick And further Wee agree that this present Writtinge shall be of full force and Authority any writings or agreements formerly made Notwithstanding And this writtinge Agreed upon March the 10th 1656/57 Is now Confirmed and Ratifyed by us whose names are hereto Subscribed the 12th day of Feb 1657

William Coddington Benedict Arnold

Signatures of major purchasers of Conanicut and Dutch Islands. Signatures appear on pages six (shown) and seven of the pre-purchase agreement. *Jamestown Historical Society (A2012.003.001).*

John Clarke, who was in England negotiating the charter that King Charles II would issue for Rhode Island five years later. It then ratifies the agreement, which was agreed to on March 10, 1656/57, but not ratified or signed until February 12 of the following year.

The document itself uses "March the 10th 1656/57" as the date of the agreement and "the 12th day of Feb 1657" as the date of ratification. The confusion is caused by Great Britain's use of March 25 as the beginning of the new year, a carryover from the Middle Ages. Since January 1 was commonly used throughout the rest of Europe, many early colonial documents recognize the ambiguity of the year by indicating both years, e.g., "March the 10th 1656/57," for dates in the period between January 1 and March 25.

A revision to the calendar introduced by Pope Gregory XIII in 1582—and by 1657 already in use in much of Europe—dropped ten days to bring the Christian calendar into conformity with the solar year. The British only adopted this change formally in 1752, when they also belatedly moved the beginning of the year from March 25 to January 1. Using the modern calendar, the date of the agreement would be March 20, 1657, and the date of the ratification would be February 22, 1658.

Chapter 2

Some Proprietors and Their Descendants

None of the sixteen members on the perpetual council appointed in the purchase agreement to oversee the governance of Jamestown and few of the larger land holders actually settled on Conanicut Island. It was the generations that followed that affected both the immediate and longer-term growth of the island.

Three of the founding families with deep roots in Jamestown are the Weedens, the Clarkes, and the Carrs.

William Weeden

William Weeden (1619–1676) signed the original pre-purchase agreement for Conanicut Island, agreeing to pay $^{1}/_{111}$ part of the total cost in exchange for the same portion of Conanicut and Dutch Islands. A $^{1}/_{111}$ part of Conanicut Island was between forty and forty-five acres, and William Weeden claimed the land on the hill rising on the north side of the Great Creek and to the east of the road that the surveyor, Joshua Fisher, had laid out bisecting the island from north to south. The farm remained in the Weeden family for almost three hundred years.

(The Weeden name does not appear on Fisher's 1658 map of the island commissioned by the proprietors. This is not unusual. Only 50 percent of

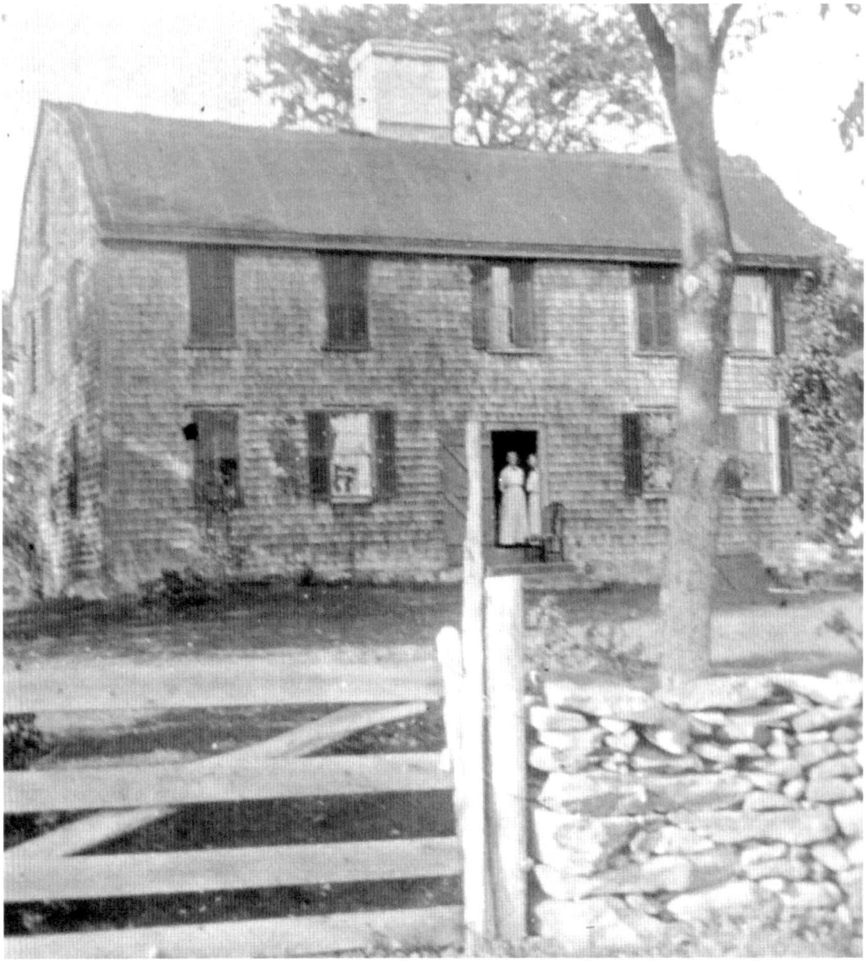

Weeden homestead in 1920. The women in the doorway are probably Lucy Ann Weeden and Elizabeth Weeden Barber. *Jamestown Historical Society (P1936.001).*

the signers are shown on the map, and the smaller the acreage, the more likely the name was to be omitted.)

Like most early proprietors, William Weeden remained in Newport and did not move to the island. He considered his property in Jamestown to be less desirable than his Newport property, and when he died in 1676, he bequeathed the forty-acre Jamestown farm to his younger son John. John (1651–1710) built a farmhouse on the south side of Weeden Lane overlooking the Great Creek and the Round Swamp. He and his wife, Jane, and their five children, John, Sarah, Jane, Daniel, and Hannah, made their home there.

John Weeden Sr. drowned in Narragansett Bay in 1710. He had prospered during his thirty-five years as a Jamestown farmer, and his estate was valued at £271.14.00, approximately $900,000 today. Apparently he kept at least one slave, since he left his "Indian Servant" Toby to his wife, Jane. He had acquired a second farm, known as "North Farm," which he willed to his older son John Jr. The family homestead—"my house and land which was given to me by my father"—John Sr. passed on to his younger son Daniel. Daniel was only fourteen when his father died, and the will instructs that "my loving Wife shall possess and enjoy my house and land which I have given to my son Daniel Weeden until he shall attain to the age of twenty-one years, Provided my wife doth continue her widowhood." The three Weeden daughters, who all married Jamestown men, each inherited about $60,000 and "one Bed with the furniture thereunto belonging."

Jamestown was flourishing in the mid-eighteenth century. A ferry to Newport was formally established in 1725, although the Carrs had been ferrying people across the East Passage at least as early as 1670. Between 1708 and 1740, the population of Jamestown had grown from 206 to 321. The percentage of the population identified as black or Native American had risen more steeply, from 15 to 30 percent. Although some of these people of non-European ancestry were free, most were slaves. When the younger John (1687–1741) died, among the bequests in his will were "a Negro man named Prince" and a "Negro boy named Robin."

Daniel (1696–1785) lived on the family homestead farm throughout his life. He married Johanna Slocum in 1720, and they had ten children. According to Weeden family lore, Daniel became known as "the old esquire" and lived many happy years at the lively family homestead. "It seems to have been a real 'Grandfather's House' where children and grandchildren met for good times and social enjoyment," wrote Mary Louise Weeden, one of Daniel Weeden Esq.'s great-granddaughters, in the late nineteenth century. "He was very fond of society and spent much money in the fashionable amusement of the day."

At seventy-eight years of age, Daniel witnessed the onset of the Revolutionary War that devastated Jamestown and destroyed the prosperity he had enjoyed. Although the farm on Weeden Lane was too far north to be affected by the burning of the village in December 1775, it could not escape the effects of the British occupation that lasted from December 1776 to October 1779. Mary Louise Weeden described her ancestor's reaction to the British occupation:

> *During the Revolutionary War, he* [Daniel Weeden] *was much annoyed by the British troops quartered near the farm on the island. Though a very old man then—and wholly unable to do any active service for his country—and when urged to leave his home and seek a less exposed place to live, he said with some energetic expressions—no—they might shoot him on his own doorsteps—as they did his cattle before his eyes—but he would never leave his house to please the British or their allies the Tories—whom he heartily despised—and knew some of his old neighbors to be.*

She goes on to describe one of the raids on the Weeden farm. Daniel's son John was seized. Daniel was tied in his chair. John's young wife stood by helplessly with their baby. John was shut in the cheese house and, with the cheese house door set slightly ajar, was forced, "with a gun covering him the while," to pass the cheeses out edgewise. After the cheeses were taken, John was hauled away by a band of Tories disguised as Indians and confined for a time on the prison ship at Newport. "The young wife and babe—and the old man—[were] left to get along as best they could with the care of the slaves, some fifteen in number young and old." After some delay, the British commander allowed John's wife, Mercy Chase, to go to her father's house in Warwick. "The old gentleman preferred to remain and was cared for during the absence of his children by a faithful slave Betty by name."

Daniel Weeden Esq. died in December 1785, three months shy of his ninetieth birthday. His will divided his land among his sons. The family homestead went to his son John (1735–1795), who was living with his family on the homestead with Daniel. Daniel Jr. (1729–1801) received confirmation of a previously gifted Jamestown tract of land plus a fifty-eight-acre farm with dwelling house that Daniel Esq. had purchased from Joseph Clarke. Son Benjamin (1731–1808) was given "use and improvement" of a house and farm in King's County, but the bequest came with a catch: the property could only pass on to "a male heir lawfully begotten of his [Benjamin's] body within wedlock." Benjamin fathered three illegitimate male offspring before his 1773 marriage to their mother. After that, only two girls were born. Daniel's daughters received money, partially in terms of forgiveness of debts owed by each daughter's husband.

Daniel Weeden Esq. manumitted his slaves in his will: "Item: I give unto my three Negro men named Ben, Tom and Tobey & my Negro woman named Betty their freedom at my decease…But if either or all of my Negros shall refuse to take their freedom my mind & will is that he, she or they so refusing shall be taken care of and supported by my executors hereafter named."

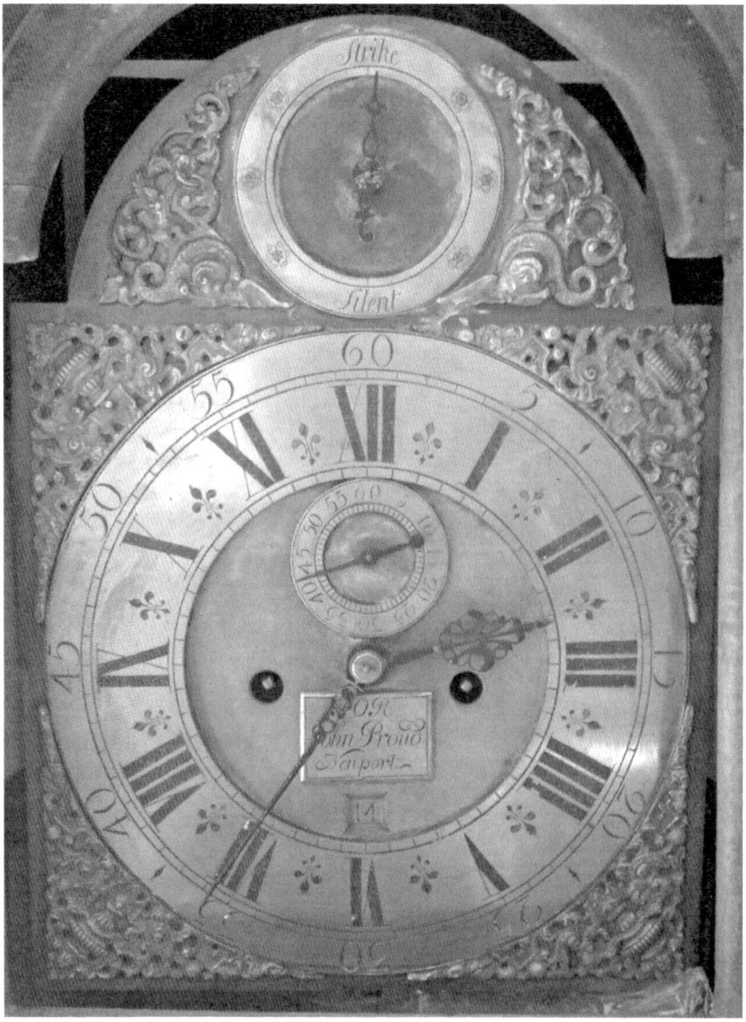

The Weeden clock, made by the Claggett clockmakers of Newport. It was first mentioned in the will of Daniel Weeden Jr. *Courtesy of Ryan Weeden.*

Presumably the "Negro woman named Betty" freed by his will was the same Betty who, according to family lore, stayed in Jamestown to care for Daniel during the British occupation of the island.

In freeing his slaves, Daniel Esq. was following the example of his son Daniel Jr., who in response to Quaker antislavery teachings had manumitted his slaves ten years earlier. In his statement of manumission, recorded on April 10, 1775, in the Rhode Island Monthly Meeting of Friends, Manumissions Book 821, after identifying the individual slave, Daniel Jr.

stated, "But I being willing to do to others as I would that others should do to me…[do] manumit release & discharge her the said Negro Girl from a State of Slavery and hereby declare her to be henceforth free as amply & fully so as if she had been born of free parents in this colony."

Daniel Jr.'s rejection of slavery did not, however, keep him from being read out of the Quaker meeting twelve years later for "attending a place of diversion, such as Musick and Dancing, and demeaning himself in other respects."

Weedens continued to be active in Jamestown life throughout the nineteenth and into the twentieth century. Damaris Weeden—a Weeden both by birth and by marriage—was the first female lighthouse keeper at Beavertail. She was appointed to the post in 1848 after the death of her husband, Robert M. Weeden, who had been the keeper since 1844. She served until 1857. Charles E. Weeden ran the Thorndike Hotel and was the first Jamestown resident to receive a telephone call when a telephone switchboard was installed there. Other Weedens moved out across the country, many keeping ties to the island.

Weedens lived on the home farm until 1924. That year Daniel Esq.'s great-great-granddaughters Lucy Ann Weeden and Elizabeth Weeden Barber sold the Weeden property and moved into the village.

JOSEPH CLARKE

Three Clarke brothers—John, Thomas, and Joseph—were among the original purchasers of Conanicut Island. Together they owned about 230 acres.

The brothers were born in Suffolk, England, to Thomas and Rose Clarke in the first two decades of the seventeenth century. Both parents died in 1627, and about ten years later, four of the siblings immigrated to the Massachusetts Bay Colony: Thomas (1605–1674), Mary (1607–1647), John (1609–1676), and Joseph (1618–1694). They were later joined by their eldest brother, Carew (1603–1679).

The family moved to Aquidneck Island with Anne Hutchinson in 1637 and the following year helped William Coddington to found Newport, where they became deeply embedded in the political life of the community.

John was the most well known of the brothers. He accompanied Roger Williams to England in 1651 to petition for a charter for the colony. When Williams returned, Clarke remained to continue the negotiations, first with the Puritan parliament of Oliver Cromwell and, after the restoration of the Stuart monarchy in 1660, with the government of the king.

Rhode Island received a very liberal Royal Charter from King Charles II in 1663. The new constitution united the four towns of Providence, Warwick, Portsmouth, and Newport into the Colony of Rhode Island and Providence Plantations. It remained the governing law of the colony and the state until 1843.

During John's long absence, his brothers Thomas and Joseph carried on his business at home. It was Joseph who acted as John's deputy on February 12, 1658, when he signed the pre-purchase agreement for Conanicut and Dutch Islands: "Joseph Clarke in the behalf of my brother Mr. John Clarke and myself." Joseph was also appointed one of sixteen members of the council to direct the governance of the two islands.

Like most of the original purchasers of Conanicut Island, Joseph continued to live in Newport. He took an active part in the government of the colony and was given the task of reviewing letters about disputes with the other colonies and of instructing his brother John concerning local decisions that affected his commission in England.

Joseph retained his Jamestown property until 1685 when he and his wife, Margaret, sold it for £101 to Francis Brinley, one of the men who had petitioned the Rhode Island General Assembly to incorporate the town of Jamestown in 1678.

Joseph was the only one of the Rhode Island Clarkes to father children who lived to maturity, and for the next six generations his descendants moved back and forth between Newport and South County. In 1886, Joseph's five-times-great-grandson Isaac Clarke and his wife, Mary Wood Soule Clarke, returned to Jamestown.

Before moving to Jamestown, Isaac Clarke had owned several icehouses at Newport's Easton Pond, the reservoir behind First Beach. In Jamestown, he continued in the same business. He and Mary purchased land to the west of Southwest Avenue where he dammed and deepened a pond to capture water from a local spring. He sold water from the spring as "Diamond Spring Water," and he stored ice cut from the pond in sawdust-insulated sheds between Southwest and Maple Avenues.

Clarke's Pond became the town's first reservoir. In June 1890, the Jamestown Light and Water Company, a private enterprise incorporated in 1888, presented the town with a plan to pump water from the pond to a standpipe on the top of the hill on Howland Avenue north of High Street. The water would flow from there down to the center of the town. Despite some opposition, the

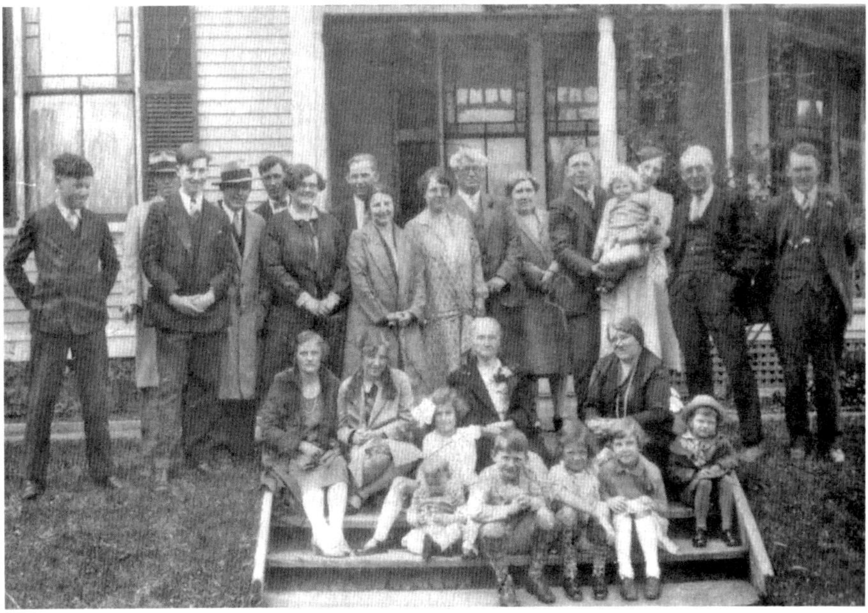

The extended Clarke family at Mary Wood Soule Clarke's eighty-fifth birthday celebration in 1928. *Jamestown Historical Society, courtesy of Ellen Arnold Brownell (P2004M.310).*

plan was accepted and a pumping station, which is now a private office building at 44 Southwest Avenue, was built just north of Isaac Clarke's ice business.

By 1900, the town's water needs had outstripped the capability of Clarke's Pond, and the private water company bought and enlarged Carr's Pond just north of Eldred Avenue, the current north reservoir.

Isaac's widow and son continued in the ice business long after his death in 1905, and Jamestown children were still skating on Clarke's Pond in the 1940s. The ice trade died when refrigerators and freezers became common appliances, and the Clarke family turned to construction, in which they are still engaged. They filled in the pond they had dug, and the water they had captured flowed into the surrounding wetlands.

CALEB CARR

Two Carr brothers were among the original proprietors. Robert (1614–1681) and Caleb (1624–1695) each purchased $^1/_{10}$ of the island, although neither ever lived on their newly acquired land.

Caleb, in particular, took an active part in Jamestown's development. In 1678, he and Francis Brinley, also one of the original proprietors, petitioned the Rhode Island General Assembly to incorporate the settlement on Conanicut Island as a town. They claimed that the new town had 150 inhabitants, which was probably more than actually resided on the island full time. On November 4, 1678, the General Assembly voted "that the said petition is granted; and that the said Quononoqutt shall be a Township, with the like priviledges and libertyes granted to New Shoreham."

Both brothers left their Conanicut Island properties to their sons. Robert's disposition of the property in his 1681 will is simple: "I give to my eldest child, Caleb Carr, all my land at Conanicut, alias Jamestown, he paying my wife £10 a year in money during her natural life."

Caleb's will was more complex. He had acquired more property in Jamestown, and he divided it among three of his sons:

> *I give and bequeath unto my son Nicholas Carr…my farm, being and lying on the island of Conanicut…forty acres of land lying on the west side of the highway, over against my brother Robert Carr, his land on the said Conanicut island, as also ten acres of land on the said island which I purchased of John Peckham, jr., and also twelve acres of land at the head of the forty acres aforesaid, which twelve acres I purchased or bought of Benedict Arnold…*
>
> *I give and bequeath unto my son Caleb Carr…the land at Conanicut, which I bought of Jirah Bull, Thomas Waterman and Richard Dunn…*
>
> *I give and bequeath unto my son Edward Carr…fifty acres and half acre of land at Conanicut, which I bought of Jeremiah Willets and sixty-five acres of land on said Conanicut island, which I bought of John Greene and Henry Bassett.*

The Carr family began the ferry service between the Conanicut and Aquidneck Islands. Caleb was providing some services between his wharf in Newport and Jamestown at least as early as 1670 when the Town of Newport awarded him £4 for "services done by him and his boat." The first recorded license for a Newport to Jamestown ferry was issued in May 1700 to John Carr, one of Caleb's younger sons. John had taken over the shipping part of the Carr businesses during his father's lifetime and under his father's will received "my whole part of Rose Island and the whole of my warehouse standing upon my wharf here in Newport." Obviously, he was expected to

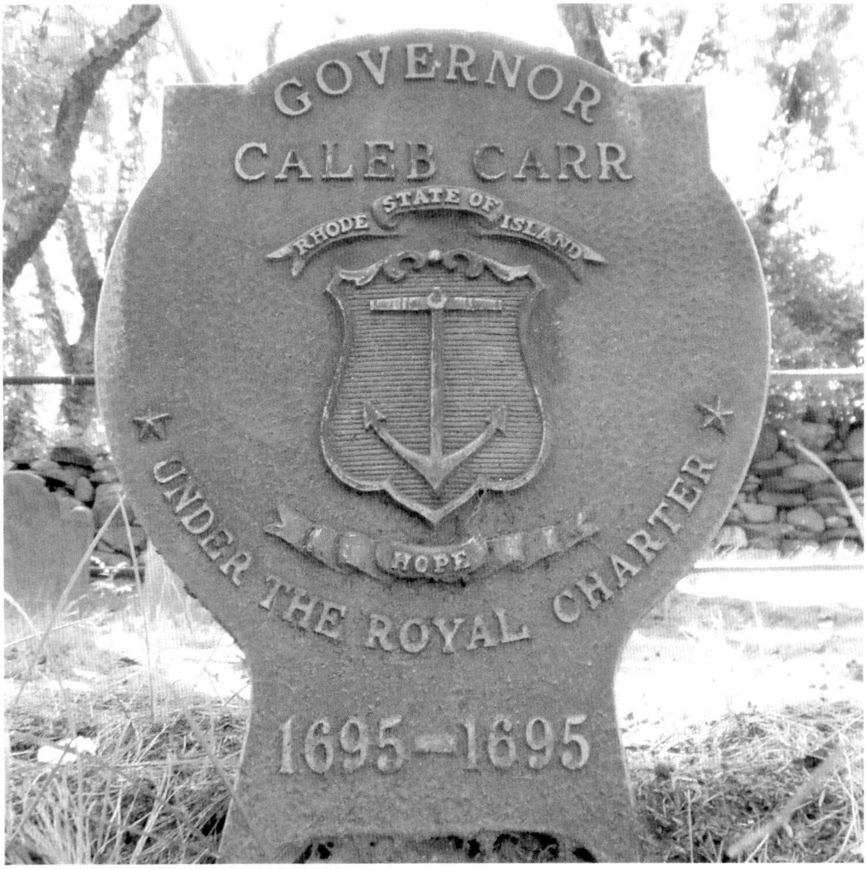

The grave of Governor Caleb Carr. Carr was originally buried in Newport; his remains were reburied in Jamestown in 1900. *Author's collection.*

work with his brother Nicholas, who under their father's will had received, in addition to the land in Jamestown, the "privilege of my wharf here in Newport, for his own occasions."

Caleb was elected governor of Rhode Island in 1695 and died later the same year when he fell (some say he was pushed) from one of his own ships on the bay.

The minutes of early town meetings are dotted with the Carr name. At the first town meeting in April 1679, Caleb Carr Sr., Caleb Carr Jr., and Nicholas Carr were elected to the four-member town council. Caleb Carr Jr. was chosen as one of two town constables. Nicholas and Caleb Carr Jr. took on the task "to be viewers of cattle, sheeps, swine, and horses which may be carried or transport from this Township."

The Carr name occurs frequently in town records throughout the colonial era. For example, the list of nine men agreeing on October 13, 1775, to stand watch against the possibility of a British landing includes six Carrs: Benjamin, Daniel, Edward, Edward Jr., John, and Samuel Jr.

Until the late nineteenth century, most of the Carrs were farmers. The Carr Homestead, which still stands on Carr Lane, was built by Caleb Carr's great-grandson Nicholas (1732–1813). According to family tradition, the house, which was the site of many Carr family gatherings over the years, stands on land that was part of the original Carr purchase and was completed in 1776.

Nicholas was a Quaker, and he remained in Jamestown during the Revolution, tilling his land. Despite his commitment to pacifism, one legend credits him with resisting the British occupation of Conanicut Island. A descendent, Walter Leon Watson, records the story in his *The House of Carr*:

> *One day as he was plowing the north lot this captain came along, and in a very insolent manner ordered him to stop his team. The command being disregarded, the captain struck him a blow on the head with his cane. Nicholas immediately declared a war of his own, and they fought the war of the revolution in miniature, and with the same result. After the captain was soundly thrashed he cried for quarter and was allowed to go on his way.*

Many of the farmers remaining on the island were Tories, and Nicholas was saved from the consequences of his action by their intervention.

As the economics of the island changed in the nineteenth century, the Carrs expanded their horizons. Isaac Carr built a store on the East Ferry wharf in 1829. With the coming of the steam ferry in the early 1870s, Carr moved his store to Narragansett Avenue, where it has since been used as a schoolhouse, a florist shop, and most recently a restaurant. The storekeeper was in his late seventies and an irascible old man when the Episcopalian congregation began the construction of a new church building at St. Matthew's in 1879. Partway through the collection that followed the laying of the cornerstone, he rose up and demanded that those present not give any money to the church if they owed anybody. "Some of you who have given money owe it to me," he shouted. "Don't give, don't give I tell you."

Isaac's grandnephew, William Lincoln Bates, who had been sent to the Providence Reform School in 1873 for stealing from Isaac's store, became a respected leader in Jamestown in the early twentieth century. Bates

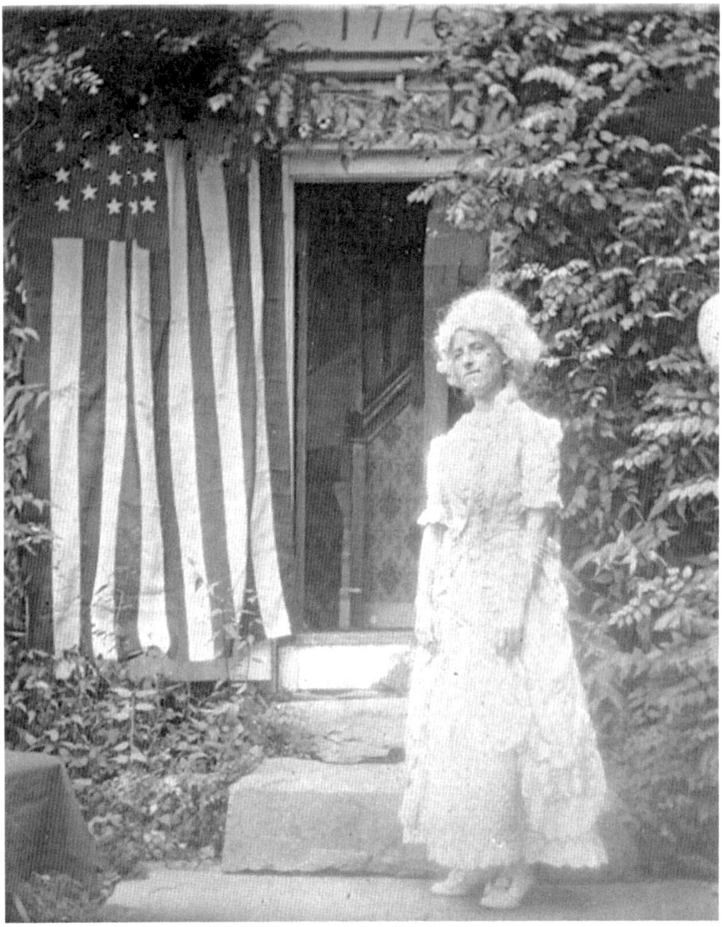

Florence Carr in 1926. The Carr family celebrated the 150th anniversary of the Carr homestead with theatricals dramatizing events in the family history. *Jamestown Historical Society (P1971.025).*

established himself as an electrotherapist in Providence in 1892 and later brought his practice to Jamestown. Like many doctors of the era, Bates did not have a medical degree, although the American Medical Association directory listed him as "Dr. William Lincoln Bates." The Dr. Bates Sanitarium on Conanicus Avenue opposite the Bay Voyage Inn was part resort, part a place for rest and recuperation, and part nursing home for the chronically ill. From 1915 through 1935, the sanitarium housed a maternity department, and at least 136 Jamestown babies were born there. Bates was one of the founding members of the Jamestown Historical Society.

Perhaps the most widely known of the late nineteenth-century Jamestown Carrs was George C[ross] Carr. His name appears again and again in town records. He reestablished the Carr connection with the ferry in 1872 when he was elected first president of the new Jamestown & Newport Ferry Company. Along with his nephew Thomas Carr Watson and a third director, Elijah Anthony, he was responsible for the purchase of the first steam-driven ferryboat for the East Passage run, the building of ferry wharfs in Newport and Jamestown, and the operation of the ferry during its first years. He was one of the developers of the Ocean Highlands plat in the Dumplings, a director of the Jamestown Light and Water Company, president of the town council, and for many years a state senator.

So many Carrs of note lived and worked in Jamestown that when the first graded school (as opposed to a one-room schoolhouse in which all grades were taught) was built in 1898, it was called simply the Carr School in honor of the family instead of one of its individual members.

Chapter 3

General Washington in Jamestown

During the 1770s, French support to the American Revolution was—despite French involvement in the Battle of Rhode Island in 1778—primarily monetary and maritime. In early 1780, King Louis XVI agreed to send both ships and land forces to the American colonies, and in July 1780, Jean-Baptiste Donatien de Vimeur, comte de Rochambeau, the French commander-in-chief, arrived in Newport with 5,800 French troops.

The French, both the men and the transports, spent the summer recovering from a rough sixty-nine-day Atlantic crossing. Rochambeau met with General George Washington in September in Hartford but returned to Rhode Island for the winter without firm plans for coordinated French-American action. Washington was in favor of trying to recapture New York, but Rochambeau wanted to bypass the British stronghold and attack the British forces farther south. Further face-to-face talks were necessary, and on Friday, March 2, 1781, Washington left his headquarters at New Windsor on the Hudson River and traveled to Newport to plan the campaign for the approaching summer.

According to the record of expenditures for the trip, Washington was accompanied by his aides, Colonel Tench Tilghman and Colonel David Humphreys, and by Major General Robert Howe. At least four other men rode with them.

The distance from New Windsor to Newport is approximately two hundred miles, and the group made good time, considering March weather and the colonial roads. Mishaps along the road delayed them a little: a horse

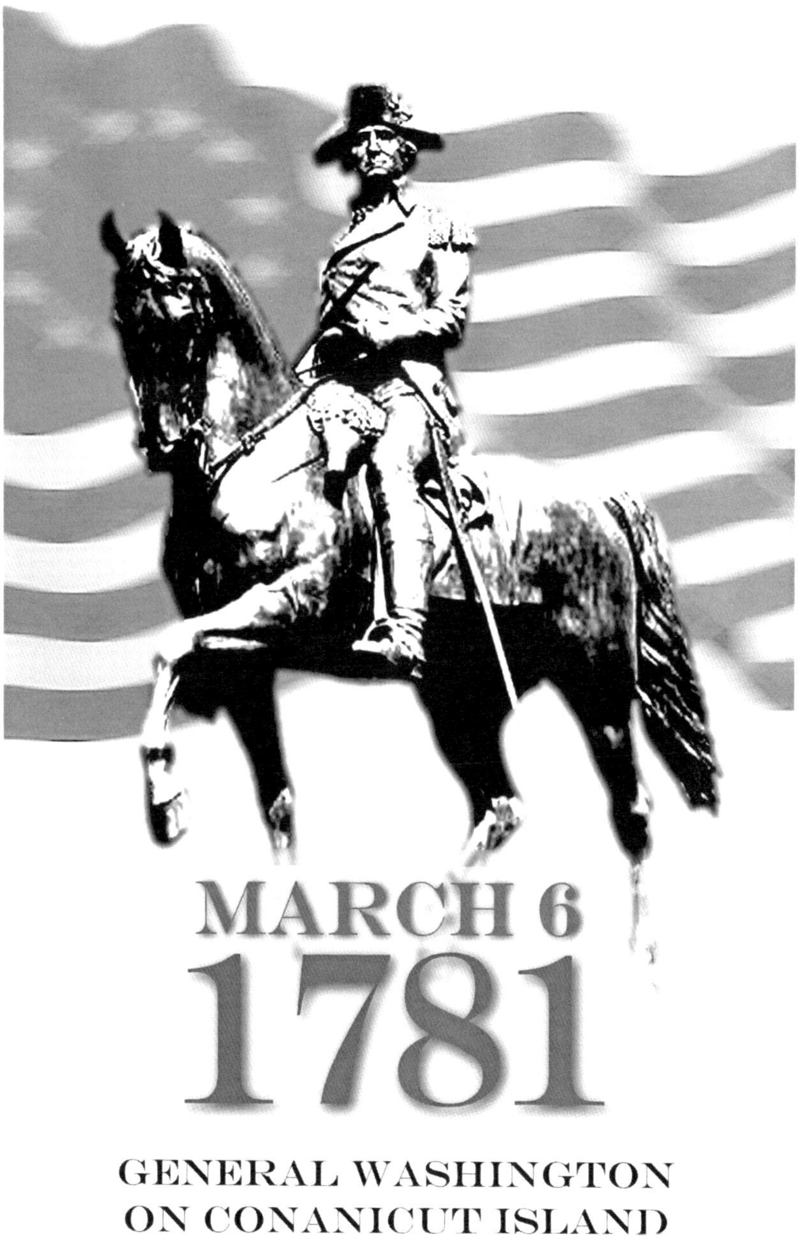

Sign on Narragansett Avenue commemorating Washington's ride across Conanicut Island in 1781. *Jamestown Historical Society (2015.109.001).*

had to be pulled out of the Housatonic River at Bull's Falls, and the rough roads forced stops to reshoe the horses. Nonetheless, Washington dined with his friend Jonathan Trumbull in Hartford on Sunday, March 4, and continued across Connecticut, arriving at Little Rest (now Kingston), Rhode Island, on March 5.

On March 6, Job Watson, who moved to Jamestown after the Revolution and became one of the largest landowners on the island, spotted Washington "with eight officers and aides as a body guard" from his watchtower on Tower Hill in South Kingstown as they rode from Kingston to Saunderstown. At Saunderstown, according to the expense account for the trip, they paid $288 to be ferried to "Connecticut," a common misnaming of the island of Conanicut.

The cost of the ferry across the West Passage was almost double what they had paid to cross the Thames River at Norwich. Mrs. French E. Chadwick, who read a paper about the trip before the Newport Historical Society in December 1912, speculated that the cost meant that no ferry was available and that a private boat was used. However, the Continental money with which Washington and his entourage paid their way was often accepted only at a deep discount, and the discount varied from place to place.

Nobody in Jamestown recorded Washington's ride from the landing at West Ferry to East Ferry. That is not strange. The British had burned down all the houses along his path in 1775. Only about 325 people lived on the island, which was still trying to recover from three years of British and Hessian occupation and deprivation.

Logic suggests that Washington and his entourage followed Ferry Road (now called Narragansett Avenue) from one side of the island to the other. At a walk, a horse would have completed the one-mile ride in about fifteen minutes. Even allowing time for debarking and re-embarking, the general's time in Jamestown was probably less than an hour.

Washington was met on the East Passage by a barge sent by Rochambeau. His arrival in Newport was recorded in the journal of Claude Blanchard, commissary of the French auxiliary army, who wrote, "This day General Washington, who was expected, arrived about two o'clock. He first went to the *Duc de Bourgogne*, [the flagship of the French fleet] where all our generals were. He then landed; all troops were under arms; I was presented to him…I mark, as a fortunate day, that in which I have been able to behold a man so truly great."

Two days later, on March 8, the *Duc de Bourgogne* and the French fleet commanded by Rear Admiral Charles René Dominique Sochet, Chevalier Destouches, left Narragansett Bay for Virginia. The action was one that

Washington had urged for some time, although his arrival in Newport probably had little to do with the preplanned action of the fleet.

Washington had evidently intended to return to East Windsor along the same route he had taken to Newport. However, during his meetings with Rochambeau, the French general had urged the necessity of Rhode Island providing more heavy guns to protect the lower bay. On March 12, Washington wrote to Rhode Island governor William Greene asking that some cannons from Providence be sent to Newport. Perhaps feeling that a visit would encourage the governor to comply, Washington ended his letter with the postscript "Since writing the foregoing letter, I have for particular reasons determined to return by the way of Providence and shall set out in the morning for that place."

On March 13, Washington left Newport, going north to Providence and then across northern Connecticut to Hartford, where he dined with Jonathan Trumbull again on March 17. He arrived back in East Windsor on March 20, as he remarked in a letter, "in the forenoon…after passing over very bad roads and riding through very foul weather without any damage."

Chapter 4

The Poor We Will Always Have With Us

Under English law still in effect in colonial and post-Revolutionary New England, each town was responsible for its own poor. Paupers—those without the financial means to supply their own needs or the ability to work to that end—could strain the resources of their community, and each community tried to protect itself from the burden in several ways.

Freemen and Inhabitants

Freemen and inhabitants were distinct groups living in a town. The concept of "freeman" was tied to gender and property. Only men could be freemen. A 1722 law defined a freeman as "a freeholder of lands, tenements or hereditaments [*sic*] in such town where he shall be admitted free, of the value of forty shillings per annum, or the eldest son of such freeholder." The value of the required freehold changed over time. Freemen of individual towns were also freemen of the colony. Freemen had the right to vote and to hold office.

An inhabitant was simply someone with the legal right to live in the town. Women, children, younger sons, and servants or slaves of freemen were inhabitants. A new arrival without the necessary holding to be a freeman could become an inhabitant by vote of the town council. When a head of household was admitted as an inhabitant, members of his family were also considered inhabitants.

Both inhabitants and freemen were entitled to town services and were guaranteed the protection of the law. To reduce the expenses associated with taking care of indigent inhabitants and to keep the need for law enforcement at a minimum, each town tried to control who was allowed to move into the town.

One of the first laws passed at the first town meeting of the "free Inhabitants of James Towne the 15th day of [April] 1679"—right after the election of town officials and the enactment of an ordinance providing for taxation—was an ordinance governing who could settle in the town, and it stated: "It is ordered and enacted that no person or persons…except it be those which are concerned in the Propriety of lands…shall have liberty to settle and inhabit in the said Towne, until such time that they are admitted by the major part of the freemen of the said Towne."

To guard against proprietors leasing their land to a person who would not be a desirable inhabitant, the law stated the "Landlord or Proprietor of the land so let or leased will give in security for his Tennant [sic] that he or they shall be no way chargeable" to the town.

Much effort was expended determining whether a new arrival would be an asset to the community. While the original 101 proprietors, or those who had bought their property from them during the intervening years, were freemen, most did not live on Conanicut Island and took little or no part in the political life of Jamestown. On May 6, 1679, soon after their election to the Jamestown Town Council, Nicholas Carr, Caleb Carr's eldest son, and Caleb Carr, the eldest son of Robert Carr, were acknowledged by the colony to be freemen of Jamestown. Both men qualified as freemen as "the eldest son of [a] freeholder."

Three freemen were admitted in April 1680: Joseph Mosie (in later records, Mosy), George Havens, and Joseph Remington. Mosie was immediately elected to the town council. The admittance of freemen by vote of the town council continued through the eighteenth century, although no complete record of their number can be found.

The first time the town council admitted a tenant as an inhabitant was at its January 1680 meeting: "George Stevens is admitted an inhabitant, upon the request of Mrs. Freeborn Hart, who hath rented him her house and land in this Towne."

Removals

With the need for permission to reside in the town came the need to remove those who came or remained without permission. This could be a long process, as the case of Martha Bristol demonstrates.

In May 1763, the town council questioned "an Indian woman named Martha Bristol [who] had illegally entered into this town" about where she had been born, who she worked for there, and how long she'd been in Jamestown, "In consequence of which examination it is Voted by the Council that the said Martha Bristol depart this town in three months…or bring such security within that time as s[ai]d Town Council shall deem sufficient for the indemnification of the town."

The following December, she still hadn't left, and the council "voted that Martha Bristol be immediately sent out of this town…to the town of Newshoreham [Block Island], the place of her last legal settlement." In May 1764, Robert Hull promised to "procure a certificate" for the woman and her family if he could, and the council voted that she "be sent out of this town in three weeks time…unless she produce a certificate or other indemnification for herself…sufficient to indemnify [the] town from any charge that may accrue by her family living therein." At the June meeting, the council voted to accept the "indemnification of Martha Bristol and her family for three years."

When the three years was up, she had to leave, and in 1768, Town Sergeant Matthew Grinold presented a bill for "transporting Martha Bristol and her family to New Shoreham" and for a boat to take them there.

Not all such removals involved Jamestown sending unwanted arrivals back to their hometowns. Jamestowners who left the island were subject to the same treatment. Freelove Howland, the daughter of a Jamestown slave who had been freed in 1775, was returned to Jamestown from Newport in 1819 and from Providence in 1842.

Overseer of the Poor

Until 1927, when the office was renamed "director of public aid" and more recently "welfare director," the overseer of the poor was responsible for enforcing removal orders and for ensuring that the young, the feeble, and the mentally impaired or disturbed were cared for.

The number of paupers needing care in Jamestown was usually not large. In general, families took care of their own. In addition, the overseer of the poor had several ways of ensuring that those who might become charges of the town did not become so.

In the case of an illegitimate child, the father was called on to provide for the child. One rather public case involved Benjamin Weeden of Jamestown and Susannah Fowler of North Kingstown. Their first son was born in 1766, and six weeks after the child's birth, the Jamestown Town Council recorded an agreement in which Benjamin agreed to pay £1,000 to Susannah and her father, Thomas. They, in turn, agreed to give security and indemnification from any charge for maintenance of the child. When the second son was born in 1771, Benjamin went to the town council to ask that the child be given to him as an apprentice. The town refused, calling the request "unprecedented and the same not warranted by any law of this colony or Great Britain, for the taking so young an infant child from the breast of the mother without her consent and binding the same by indenture to the person who is or may be charged with begetting of it." Susannah and Benjamin finally married in 1773.

Apprenticeship was a second way of ensuring that orphaned or indigent children did not become dependent on public aid. Thomas Howland, a

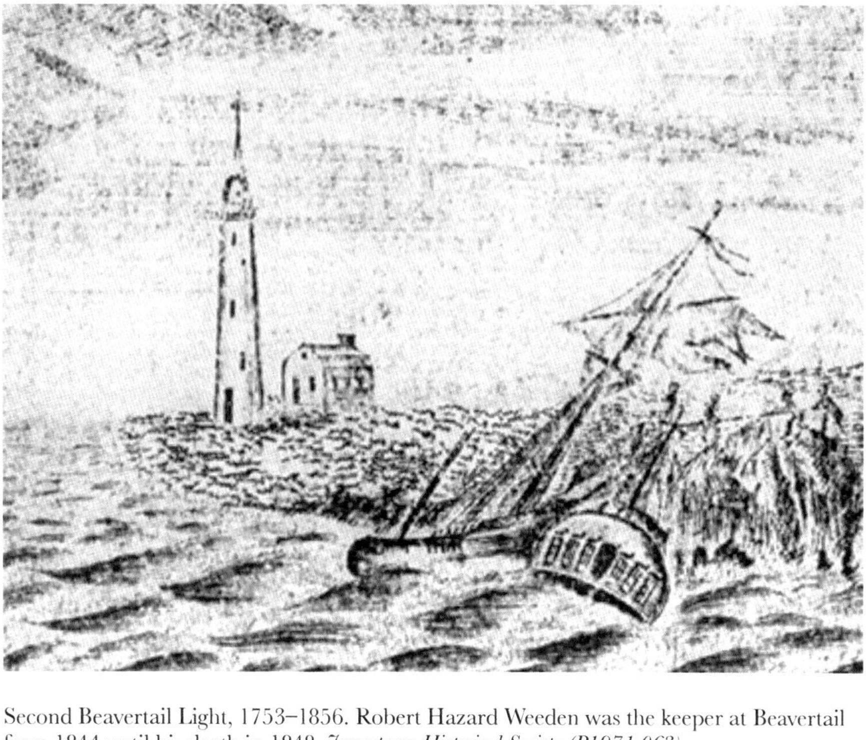

Second Beavertail Light, 1753–1856. Robert Hazard Weeden was the keeper at Beavertail from 1844 until his death in 1848. *Jamestown Historical Society (P1971.063).*

nephew of Freelove Howland, the woman returned to Jamestown as an indigent, was apprenticed when he was five years old to Robert Hazard Weeden. Indentures were legal contracts, involving serious commitments on both sides:

> *This Indenture Witnesseth that John Remmington, Overseer of the Poor of the Town of Jamestown...do place and bind out as an apprentice a poor Child, a free Black named Thomas Howland son of Patience Howland of said town of Jamestown who is lawfully settled in and became chargeable to said town who is thought by said Overseer to be unable to maintain himself unto Robert H. Weeden of Jamestown aforesaid to learn the art, trade, and mystery of a Farmer.*

Robert, who was later the keeper of the Beavertail light, in turn committed to "teach and instruct the said apprentice...in the art, trade or calling of a farmer and by the best way or means he can also to teach and instruct the said apprentice...to read, write and cipher as far as the rule of three...and provide for the said apprentice, good and sufficient meat, drink, Clothing, lodgings and other necessities." (The "rule of three" is a method for calculating ratios of the form "a" is to "b" as "c" is to "x" when "x" is an unknown quantity and the other values are known.)

Benjamin Underwood: Debtor

Until after the Civil War, debtors in Rhode Island could be imprisoned for defaulting on their obligations. One case from the immediate post–Revolutionary War period is particularly poignant.

Benjamin Underwood was born in Jamestown about forty years before the Revolution began. He was a farmer and—by his record—a civic-minded patriot. He was elected town clerk (1760–82), town warden (1768–73, 1776–81), and representative to the General Assembly in 1776. He was a captain in the Newport County militia regiment from 1761 to 1776 and recruiting officer in 1777 and 1780.

When the British occupied Conanicut Island in 1776, Underwood fled with his wife and six children to the mainland. When he returned after the occupation ended in 1779, he found his house uninhabitable and his farm a wasteland.

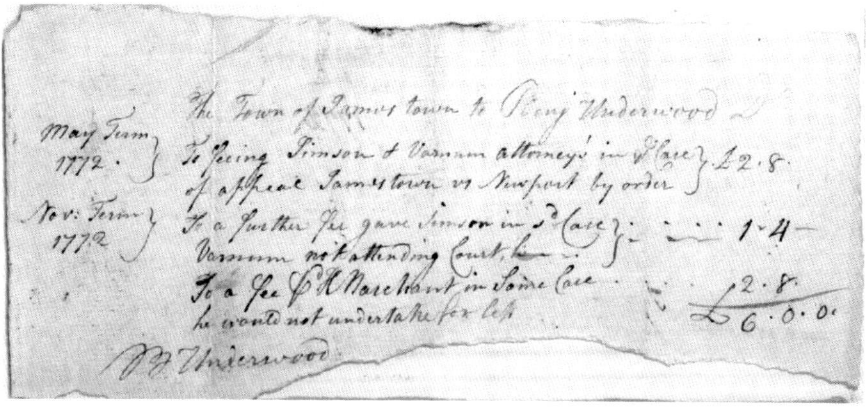

Invoice to the town from Benjamin Underwood, November 1772. Underwood billed the town £6 for services during the previous six months. *Jamestown Historical Society (T2007.045.002).*

He tried to recover. The town owed him about £91—between $9,000 and $11,000 today—for his services as town clerk and in the General Assembly. In 1780, he received about a quarter of the amount owed him. Samuel Babcock of South Kingstown lent him—perhaps had lent him earlier while he was living off-island—a sum approximately equal to the amount still owed him as town clerk.

In August 1781, Babcock sued for payment of the debt. Since Underwood was unable to repay the loan, he was imprisoned in Newport until he could.

Underwood languished in prison for fifty-three months, writing legal petitions for other prisoners and building wooden boxes and pails to get cash for food, since at this period prisoners were not fed by the government. During his imprisonment, he kept a diary of which four pages, documenting twenty-four days of his life, have survived. Finally, in 1786, he petitioned the General Assembly that he "be discharg'd from the Contracts on which held and become a more Useful Citizen to the State." The General Assembly released him and gave him three years to repay his debt.

He died a pauper sometime in 1790.

Chapter 5

Conanicus Spring

Until the 1870s, Jamestown was a land of farmers. According to the 1783 agricultural census, most of the town's forty families lived on one of its thirty-three farms. While some of the farms were as large as 500 acres, the average size was about 150 acres. Ten were smaller than 50 acres.

One of the smallest farms was owned by John Tew. His 14-acre farm on the west side of North Main Road was a small portion of the land his ancestor Richard Tew and Richard's son-in-law Samuel Billings had bought in 1657. Originally Tew held 88 acres and Billings claimed 16. In 1679, Tew purchased another 16 acres for which he paid "one good ewe and six ewe lambs," an unusual barter agreement even in those days. When Billings's heirs deeded their land to the Tews in 1690, it increased the Tew family's total holding to 120 acres.

Over the next century, the Tews bought, sold, and divided among themselves land that overlooked what is now the north reservoir but was then the much smaller Carr's Pond.

Information gleaned from the 1783 agricultural census draws a picture of John Tew's life. Most of his land was pasture. The two acres he tilled produced fifty bushels of grain—probably white flint Indian corn. He worked the farm pretty much alone, except for what help his twenty-six-year-old wife, Hannah—if we infer correctly from the tombstones in the Tew burial ground on the farm—could give. He had no slaves, nor did he have sons old enough to vote or be taxed separately. He owed nobody anything. His total worth was $109—$100 in land and $9 in personal property.

What he did have on his property was Conanicus Spring, one of the twenty-three natural springs on Conanicut Island that were identified by Richard Champlin in the *Jamestown Press* in 1993. The spring, which fed into Carr's Pond, made it possible for him to water his cows and to chill the milk they produced. A second house on the east side of North Main Road, which has since disappeared—probably when the reservoir was built in 1900—also depended on the spring.

Until at least 1827, some of the original Tew farm remained in the family, but by 1844, Walter Watson—a descendant of Job Watson, who arrived on the island about 1784 and by 1800 was the largest landowner in Jamestown—had acquired 160 acres of Tew land. He left his son William eighty acres of the parcel, and in 1857 William Watson built a house and barn on the hill above the spring south of the Tew burial ground.

William's farm remained in the Watson family until 1942, although pieces were sold off, and by 1943 the farm itself had been reduced to forty-seven acres.

Domingo Souza (in some records the last name is Vigaro) and his wife, Frances, leased the remaining farmland and moved into the old Watson farmhouse. Souza was an immigrant from the Azores, and like many Portuguese immigrants to Jamestown, he spoke little English. His wife, Frances, was the daughter of Joseph Martin, who had emigrated from the Azores a generation earlier. She had grown up on Beavertail Farm, which her father rented from the Wharton family. Joseph Martin was remembered affectionately by many Jamestowners for his generosity during the Great Depression of the 1930s. At the farm, he grew most of his own food, and he shared his milk and vegetables liberally with poor families free of charge.

For over twenty years, the Souzas worked the small farm, much as John Tew had. Domingo had a herd of cows, and he sold their milk to Anderson's Dairy. According to local lore, he trained his cows to come when he called them. He would stand on the ridge behind his house, put his hands on his hips, and yell for them. And they came. Frances grew vegetables. Most of the produce was consumed or canned, but some was sold.

They also occasionally boarded horses for summer people in the village. One young girl—young, that is, in the 1940s—remembers walking the two miles from her home at West Ferry in the summer to ride the horse she kept with them. She was delighted one spring to return and discover that the Souzas had acquired a new horse and had named it after her.

In 1964, the Souzas—then in their sixties—moved into the village, and the farm was once again divided. In 1966, George Hodges bought the old

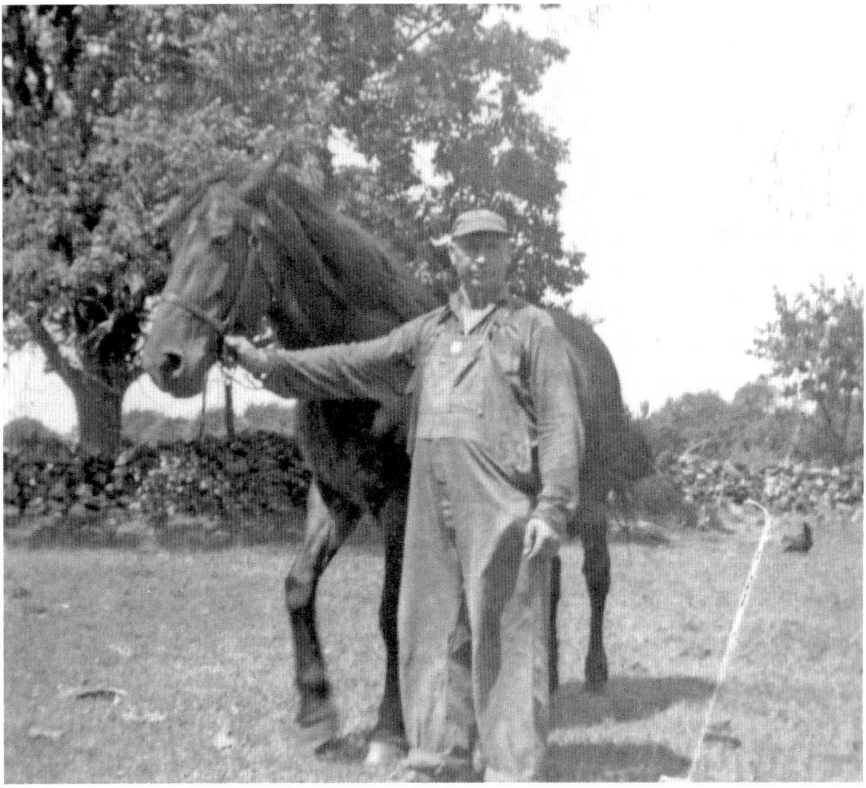

Domingo Souza on the farm at Conanicus Spring. *Courtesy of Emeline Cabral and Mary Greene.*

Watson farmhouse and four surrounding acres and called his property Red Wing Hill Farm. Hodges ran Pitchers, a store at East Ferry. In his spare time, he raised vegetables on the small farm and sold them at his vegetable stand near Conanicus Spring.

The current owners of the spring have cleared away the debris of years and found a small pool dammed around the spring proper and a larger pool below. Both pools had been lined with flat stones by the farmers who used them. Watercress still grows abundantly around the pool edges.

Part II
DEVELOPMENT

Chapter 6

Real Estate Dan

John Fitch constructed steamboats capable of plying inland waterways as early as 1785. Robert Fulton's *Clermont* steamed from New York City to Albany in 1807, averaging about five miles per hour. Starting in 1822, steamboats regularly carried passengers up and down Narragansett Bay from Providence to Newport and on to New York City.

Fifty years later, Jamestown still depended on sail ferries. According to "An Old Resident" writing in the *Newport Daily News* in 1902, "The [sail] ferry had been run largely for the benefit of the islanders, and was regarded as a sort of family or neighborhood arrangement" and not as a for-profit business. No one off island seemed to think that providing a more reliable service for the four hundred people who lived on the island would be profitable.

But times were changing. In the spring of 1872, Jamestowners decided that if they wanted modern transportation to and from the island, they had to do it themselves. They formed the Jamestown & Newport Ferry Company with the town owning 60 percent of the stock in the company. The steam ferry *Jamestown*—the first of four ferryboats with that name—was put in service on the Newport-Jamestown route in 1873.

Almost immediately, land that for almost two hundred years had been farmed by a small number of local families became valuable as house lots. In 1875, there were only 103 houses on the island, housing 488 permanent residents. By 1895, the population had increased over 60 percent to 813. More dramatically, the number of houses had more than tripled, and almost 50 percent of the 325 single-family dwellings were unoccupied in the winter months.

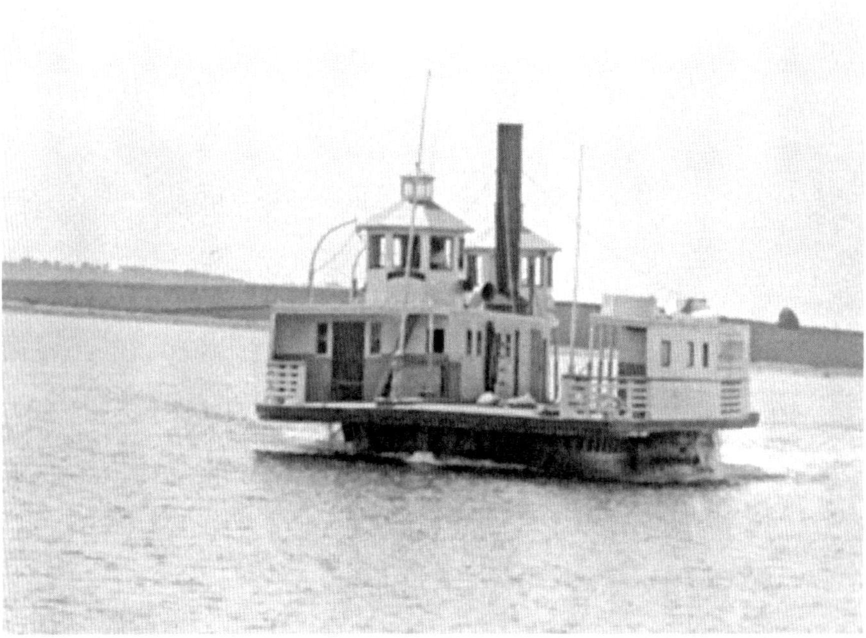

Jamestown (I). The ferry was in service on the East Passage from 1873 to 1888 and on the West Passage from 1888 to 1893. *Jamestown Historical Society (P1980.186).*

Hotels grew up around the new ferry wharf. By the 1890s, the hotels and boardinghouses in the village could accommodate over one thousand visitors.

Along with land development came the new-to-Jamestown profession of real estate agent. One of the most prominent real estate agents in this early stage was Daniel Watson, colloquially known as "Real Estate Dan."

Daniel was the seventh of the ten children of Dr. Daniel and Sarah G.C. (Arnold) Watson of Newport. The Watson family had a long history in Jamestown. Daniel's great-grandfather Job Watson (1744–1812) came to Conanicut Island from South County soon after the American Revolution. He and his five sons acquired large tracts of land—including all the farms on the west side of North Road from Eldred Avenue to Narragansett Avenue—and took an active part in the political life of the town.

Daniel Watson grew up in Newport, and on the eve of the War Between the States (1861–65), he was living there with his parents on Spring Street. Like virtually all young men in their twenties, he registered for the draft, and he served as a hospital steward on several vessels in the Union fleet blockading southern ports during the war. In the early 1870s, he began dividing his time between

Newport and Jamestown, developing a successful career selling Jamestown's newly subdivided farms.

The first development in Jamestown village was Ferry Meadows, platted in 1873 near the new wharf at East Ferry on a farm that had belonged to John Howland. Watson sold some of the lots there but shared responsibility for developing the plat with other sales agents. The next year, 1874, Watson's cousin Thomas Congdon Watson divided his land near West Ferry, creating the Bay View development. Daniel Watson was made sole agent to sell the Bay View lots. The following year, Watson published a large map of Jamestown showing the subdivisions and advertising his responsibility for them.

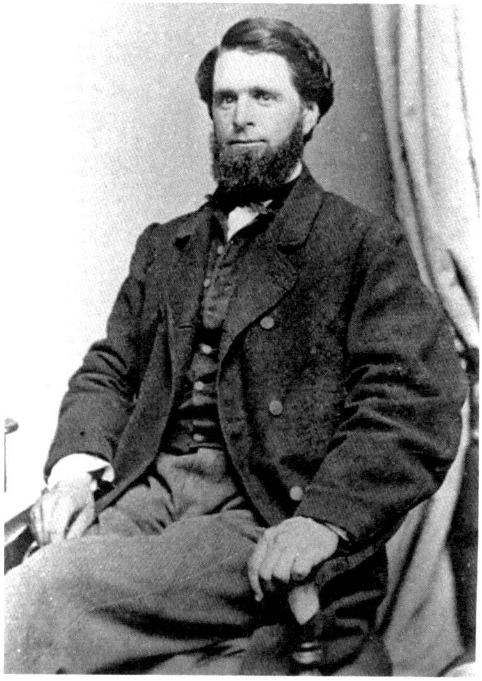

Thomas Congdon Watson, the first developer to give "Real Estate Dan" total responsibility for selling the lots in his subdivided farm. *Jamestown Historical Society (P1976.099).*

Over the next twenty-five years, Watson was named sole sales agent for every major development in Jamestown south of the Great Creek.

The Ocean Highlands Company was organized in 1875 to develop the Dumplings area. The plat contained about two hundred acres, many of them on rocky coastline with splendid views. Transportation into the area was difficult, and development of the Dumplings proceeded slowly. The first house was not built there until 1881. Then, in 1883, Watson teamed up with the Shingle-style architect Charles L. Bevins, bringing Bevins commissions for houses that were uniquely suited to the rough terrain and in the process speeding the development of the area. Bevins and Watson worked together until Watson's death.

The Bryer farm encompassed land on both sides of Conanicus Avenue north of Jamestown harbor. When it was platted in 1884, Daniel Watson became involved in development of commercial as well as residential sites. In 1889, the Champlin House, later know as Maplewood or Cottage Number

2 of the Dr. Bates Sanitarium, was built on the west side of Conancius Avenue. The same year, the Bay Voyage Inn was floated across the bay from Middletown to its site between the Champlin House and the water. Shoreby Hill development began two years after the Bryer farm was platted, and Daniel Watson was given the responsibility for finding buyers for the lots.

The final development for which Watson took the lead was Ocean View, which subdivided the old South Beavertail Farm and included much of what is now Beavertail State Park. The plat was recorded in 1899, and Watson did not live to see the development to fruition. He died on June 13, 1899, at age sixty-two, while showing a client land in the Dumplings. He left behind his wife, the former Susan E. Commerford of Newport, whom he had married only eleven years earlier. They had two little girls, and at his death, his wife was pregnant with their third daughter.

Chapter 7

Shoreby Hill

When summer vacationers "discovered" Jamestown in the 1870s and 1880s, farms surrounded the tiny village at the ferry wharf. Only a block north of Ferry Road (now Narragansett Avenue) lay the fifty-eight-and-a-half-acre Greene farm. At the center of the farm, near the top of the rise above Jamestown Harbor, stood the seventeenth-century Greene farmhouse, the only pre-Revolutionary building left standing in or near the village after the destructive British raid of December 1775.

The land had been farmed by the Greene family from the early eighteenth century until the death of Joseph Greene Jr. in 1839. Greene had no children, and his will placed the farm in perpetual trust for the benefit of those who believed in Greene's particular form of Quakerism.

For over fifty years, the Quakers continued to work the land as the village grew to the south. In 1891, the Rhode Island Supreme Court declared Greene's will invalid on the grounds that it was impossible to know what a person truly believed. The Quakers decided it was the right time to sell.

The Jamestown Land Company—formed in 1895 by St. Louis residents Ephron Catlin, James Taussig, his son Charles S. Taussig, and Henry Scott, along with Charles Acton Ives, a prominent Newport political figure—bought the Greene farm for $75,000 (approximately $2 million in 2015 dollars). Catlin and the Taussigs weren't newcomers to Jamestown. The families had summered on the island for several years, and Catlin owned a house on Friendship Street. They worked with local realtor Daniel "Real Estate Dan" Watson to buy the land and to sell the lots that were platted on it.

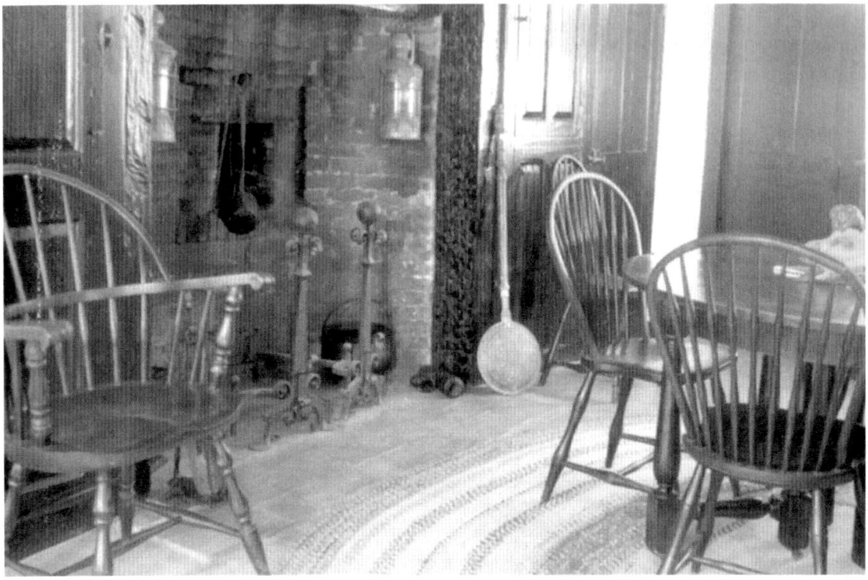

The colonial Greene farmhouse near the top of Shoreby Hill. *Jamestown Historical Society (P1976.039).*

To transform the farmland into a sophisticated and exclusive vacation enclave, modeled on private "garden suburbs" in St. Louis, the company hired Ernest W. Bowditch, who had recently designed the private community of Tuxedo Park, New York. Bowditch's design embodied the distinctive characteristics of late-nineteenth and early-twentieth-century suburban planning theories. It featured curved roads that followed the contour of the land and afforded maximum visibility of the waterfront. The lots varied in size but averaged about a quarter acre. Stone pillars at each entrance to the development created an air of exclusivity. The Greene farmhouse was kept as a residence for a manager to maintain the common property and keep an eye on the empty houses during the winter.

The developers invested about $125,000 in infrastructure for the private community. The general contractor, Thomas F. Mague, hired Italian laborers from Boston—at times as many as one hundred—who lived in temporary quarters that have long since disappeared. They buried sewer pipes two feet in diameter to carry raw sewage far out into the bay (a common practice at the time) and laid six-inch water mains. They graded and macadamized streets and built gravel sidewalks. Trees and plants began arriving in late April 1896, and William Bryan, a landscape gardener from New Jersey, directed their planting.

By September 1896, the construction was far enough along for sales of lots to begin. Lot price varied with location and view. The lots on Alden Road at the top of the green on the eastern slope of the hill were offered for $0.35 to $0.40 per square foot, or about $6,000.00 each. Middle-of-the-block lots without a water view could be as inexpensive as $0.04 a square foot.

Purchasers were constrained by deed to follow the rules of the planned community. Only one building, costing no less than $3,000, could be built on each lot. It was to be set back at least twenty feet from the road and used exclusively as a private residence. No hedges fronting the road could be higher than three and a half feet. A covenant, similar to those used by condominiums today, ensured that the roads and other common areas would be maintained.

The land company, which owned the land down to the water's edge, built a bulkhead to protect the hill from erosion and sold a fifty-foot-wide strip along it to the town for one dollar after the town agreed to build and maintain what is now Conanicus Avenue. Along the bulkhead, a boardwalk extended out over the beach. A pier in the middle, added two years later, reached three hundred feet into the bay.

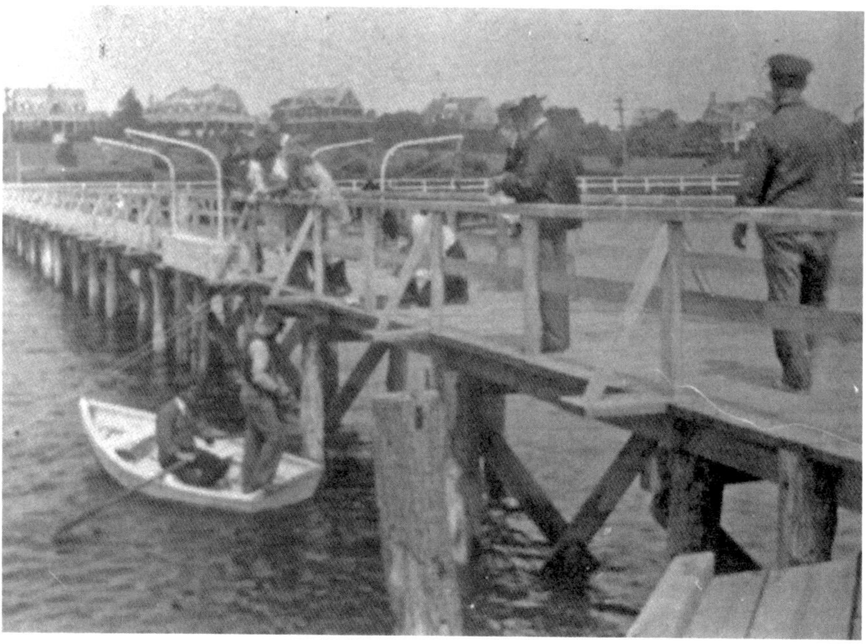

The Shoreby Hill pier. The Shoreby Hill green and the boardwalk are seen in the background. *Jamestown Historical Society (P1978.076).*

The First Subdivision of Shoreby Hill, also called Lower Shoreby, was legally recorded with the Town of Jamestown in September 1898, and the first homes were ready for occupancy that summer. The houses clustered around the green and meadow at Shoreby Hill's east entrance. The families who summered in them came from St. Louis; most lived on or near the exclusive Vandeventer Place there.

Among the first houses completed were the three distinctive homes that stand at the top of the Shoreby Hill green and field overlooking Narragansett Bay. The farthest north was built by Edward Mallinckrodt of St. Louis. Mallinckrodt and his brothers had founded a company in 1867 that was to become, by the time of his death in 1928, a vast chemical and pharmaceutical corporation. It is now the Mallinckrodt Group, Inc. James Taussig, a St. Louis attorney and one of the developers of Shoreby Hill, built the center house. The house's relaxed Colonial Revival style was likely considered by Taussig to be a model to suggest ease and relaxation to potential buyers of lots. The Red House on the south was built by Henry and Margaret Lionberger Potter. Potter's career in St. Louis ranged from selling hay and grain to, at the time of his death, being the president of the St. Louis Steel Barge Company. Mrs. Potter was the sister of Mrs. Davis at 40 Emerson Road.

Eight more houses—including the Shoreby Hill Club, which was built as a dining pavilion and a social club for Shoreby Hill families—were built almost immediately. No more houses were completed until the Second Subdivision of Shoreby Hill, known as Upper Shoreby, was recorded by the town in 1911.

In 2012, the district of Shoreby Hill was added to the National Register of Historic Places. The nomination called it "an exceptional example in Rhode Island of a planned Garden Suburb."

Chapter 8

Summer Cottages for Rent

With the development of reliable steam ferry transportation across the East Passage in 1873 and across the West Passage fifteen years later, Jamestown became a summer destination and resort.

Initially, simple accommodations were available in ferry houses and boardinghouses. Because many summer visitors were accustomed to a more sophisticated lifestyle, hotels were built to accommodate them. The Bay View Hotel was built in 1873, followed by the Gardner House, the Thorndike Hotel, the Bay View House (as the large Bay View tower was called), the Bay Voyage Inn, and several smaller hotels, all of which operated on the "American Plan." The lodging package included rooms or suites, three meals a day, and often laundering, tailoring, entertainment, and even, according to bills that have survived, the occasional loan of cash to visitors without local banking facilities.

Many visitors spent the entire summer season in Jamestown. Then, as now, longer-term visitors often preferred a more home-like environment and built cottages, which ranged from one-room beach houses to large elaborate mansions.

Developers also built cottages specifically as rentals. Some of the developers were prominent Jamestowners. John J. Watson, town clerk and owner of Thorncroft at 175 Narragansett Avenue, built Hedgerow at 16 Green Lane in 1888 and rented out rooms in both places. He also used Hedgerow as the town clerk's office in 1889. William H. Knowles, the owner of the Bay View Hotel, owned Shore Cottage, across from the hotel next to

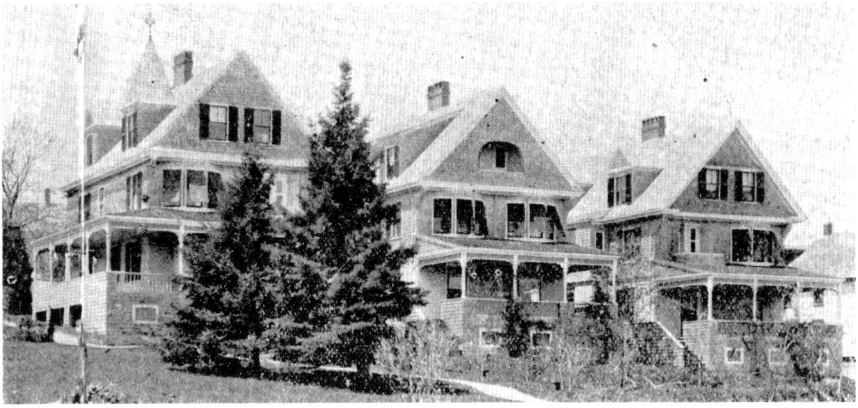

The Three Sisters on Conanicus Avenue. Families living in them enjoyed hotel privileges at the Thorndike Hotel. *Jamestown Historical Society (A2007.073.018).*

what is now Veterans Square. Patrick H. Horgan, a developer from Newport who built the Thorndike Hotel on the site where BankNewport now stands, also built cottages to rent on his property near the hotel. The best known of Horgan's cottages are the Three Sisters on Conanicus Avenue, named after his daughters Betty, Nina, and Myra. Families who rented cottages owned by Horgan enjoyed hotel privileges at the Thorndike. A very successful developer, Horgan was the largest owner of real estate in Newport when he died in 1932.

Although many summer rentals were built specifically for summer use, others were the winter homes of year-round residents. A family would rent its home to members of the summer colony and find other accommodations for the season. Occasionally, they would spend the summer with friends, as the Al Richardson family did in 1937. More often, Jamestowners had a second home on the island and "camped out" there. The Ferdinand Armbrust family, for example, rented out their house on Shady Lane and stayed at Rest-a-Bit, a smaller but still comfortable cottage, on the shore at Potter's Cove.

The amenities at the cottages varied greatly. Watson's Hedgerow had fourteen rooms with one bath. It rented for $500 for the summer of 1901. ($1 was equal to about $26 today.) The Three Sisters, built in 1897, each had twelve rooms, one bath, and two toilets and rented for $500 eleven years later. The 1912 advertisement for the Three Sisters includes the information that they had no garages—a new consideration reflecting the impact that the automobile was having on Jamestown.

That same year, the Gibson cottage at 55 Grinnell Street rented for $125. The cottage had five rooms and no bath or toilet. The Gibson cottage had been built a few years earlier by Percival Gibson for his own use. Gibson had been orphaned at the age of fifteen and "put" in the navy. When he was discharged, he became a carpenter, working on many fine houses in Newport, including the Breakers. The house remained a rental for only a short period. Gibson died in 1916, and in 1924, Colonel and Mrs. Thomas Kirkpatrick purchased the Gibson home as a summer residence. In 1938, the house became the summer home of Dr. Julius F. Neuberger, a retired U.S. Navy captain.

Other houses were rented only occasionally. Beachhaven at 141 Conanicus Avenue was designed by Charles L. Bevins for Dr. David Kindleberger in 1886. He and his wife summered in Jamestown until her death in 1898, but that year, he rented it out.

At the beginning of the twenty-first century, without the large residential hotels that characterized the resort one hundred years ago, summer rentals in Jamestown are at a premium. About one hundred houses are rented out each summer. Most—about 80 percent—are owned by people from out of state, many of whom live in the house for part of the summer and rent it only when they are not using it. The balance of rental houses are owned by Jamestowners who either summer at a second home, generally off-island, or live on their boats for the summer or travel during the weeks their house is rented.

The majority of visitors now rent by the week or month rather than for the whole summer season. The rentals offer, on the average, one bathroom for every two bedrooms, and rents range from $1,500 a week for a modest cottage to $20,000 for a large oceanfront house with a pool.

The most frequent question asked by prospective renters is, "Does the house have Wi-Fi?"

Chapter 9

The First Portable House

The first portable house to be erected in Jamestown is being put up for Mrs. Sharrer of Wilmington, N.C., on her lot on the west ferry.
—Newport Daily News, *August 19, 1896*

That report may surprise those who are under the impression that portable houses, or prefabs, are a comparatively recent innovation, dating back to the pre-cut buildings offered in the early mail-order catalogues. In fact, their history is a good deal longer—more than two hundred years.

As early as the late 1700s, English and American firms supplied prefabricated houses to locations where shelter was needed quickly or where building materials or skilled labor were not easy to come by, such as new colonies or settlements. Some of the first clients were English missionaries as they carried their civilized way of life as well as their religion to "benighted heathen lands." The earliest of these ready-made homes were manufactured in the old-fashioned way, one house at a time, first constructing it and then disassembling it and shipping the parts to the new destination. It was not a very economical procedure that soon gave place to more practical ways to get the job done.

As the dawning industrial age brought new technologies and new methods of manufacture, the craftsman with his handsaw and plane began to be replaced by the factory worker. Well-designed mail order, or kit, houses became cheaper and more efficient, with less wastage, and a number of firms set themselves up in business. The 1848 California gold rush provided a tremendous boost to the industry. According to some estimates, five thousand houses were shipped from the northeastern states around the Horn to satisfy the need for shelter in the newly populated areas on the West Coast. Later in the century, as the railroad network spread, new demands from the growing numbers of settlers in the prairie states provided additional stimuli.

The owner of the first portable house in Jamestown, Jeannette Sharrer, was the widow of a naval officer and the mother of two children. Her husband had bought land in Jamestown in 1887—lot sixty-two on the Bay View plat, 20,530 square feet of shore property overlooking the West Passage. It had cost $400. He died two years later at the early age of forty-two.

In 1896, with her children grown, Mrs. Sharrer was ready to build a summer home for herself on the lot she had inherited. Nothing elaborate—just a small house where she could watch the view over the water, the ferry going back and forth, and the sunsets. A portable house would be just the thing. It could be put up more quickly than anything a local builder could construct, and probably more cheaply.

On January 4, 1887, William M. Ducker of New York acquired patent number 355,441 for his method of construction, and the Ducker Portable

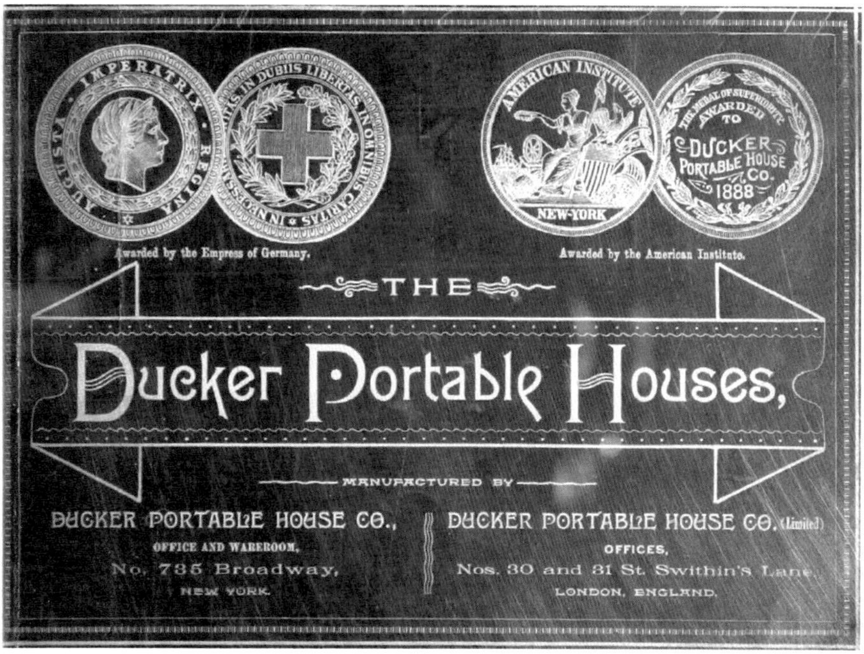

Ducker Portable House Co. catalogue. Jeannette Sharrer ordered "Style No. 14" for her Jamestown cottage. *Jamestown Historical Society.*

House Company established offices in New York and London and a manufacturing plant in Factoryville, Pennsylvania. As well as houses of various sizes, the company made lawn pavilions, bathhouses, billiard rooms, stables, and other specialized buildings, even larger structures such as administration buildings and hospitals. A catalogue dating from this period described its offerings in most attractive terms:

> *The Ducker Portable Buildings are light, durable, well ventilated, warm in winter, cool in summer, healthful and cheap. They can be erected and taken down with ease and quickness, and, taking into consideration their size and accommodation, their cost will be found to be less than any other portable building yet invented. They are built in sections (which open and close) for facility of transportation, and are put up without the use of nails, screws or any external appliance whatever.*

The construction technique featured wall panel sections that were hinged together. Where in ordinary construction nails or screws would be used, bolts were inserted through predrilled holes and tightened with wing nuts, so no screwdriver, spanner, or wrench was needed.

On July 24, 1896, Mrs. Sharrer placed her order with the Ducker Portable House Company for a portable house, "Style No. 14, according to the following specifications:"

> *Main house size: 17 feet by 22 feet with a kitchen extension 8.3 feet by 11 feet.*
>
> *Veranda across the front of the house 10 feet wide, extending around one corner 5 feet 6 inches.*
>
> *Veranda with lattice enclosure across rear of house, 5 feet wide beginning where the kitchen joined the main house.*
>
> *Four doors, one of which to be divided in half (Dutch), and one blind door as shown in the catalog.*

In addition, the order included four folding tables, a vegetable bin, cupboard, two terra-cotta chimney pieces, and an "earth closet." The earth closet (privy) was not attached, of course, so that it could be put up in a suitably private place.

This was clearly not a complete description, as there is no mention of windows and shutters, which were included in the delivered house, nor of one of the advertised features of Ducker buildings described in its catalogue:

a bed hinged to one of the wall panels that could be folded up in the daytime to convert a bedroom into a living room. The house must have been equipped with this since it was essentially a one-room cottage. Delivery was promised within thirty days.

No account exists of the arrival of the house at its chosen site or of the process of erecting it, presumably under the supervision of "our man" who was in charge of the consignment. According to the catalogue, "two men can erect the building on ordinary ground in two hours." Although the ground on the West Passage lot could hardly be classified as ordinary, "inequalities of the ground are provided for by adjustable feet attached to the side sections of the floor."

Mrs. Sharrer paid the Ducker Company $570 for her house, but of course this was not her only expense. Steps up to the front porch had to be made, and a chimney had to be built. She engaged T.C. Dowling of North Road, "Carpenter & Builder" and formerly from Newport, to do this work. His first bill for $39.80 was probably for the steps. Work on the chimney began on

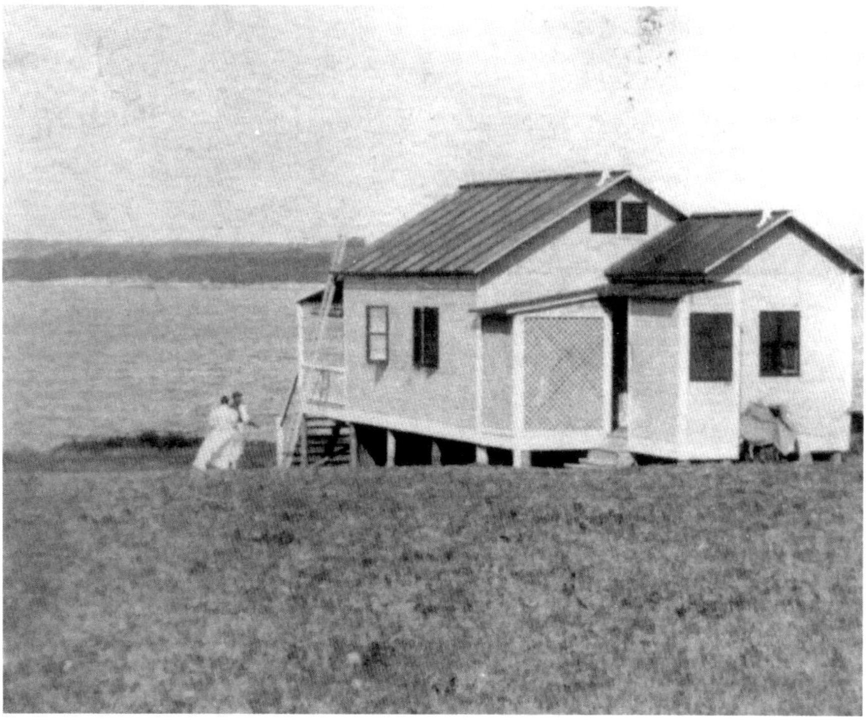

The Sharrer cottage with the West Passage and Dutch Island beyond. *Courtesy of the Daggett family.*

October 3 and took a week. The bill for that came to $206.27. (The itemized account shows that the skilled workmen employed as masons earned $3.50 per day.) A well was dug to the southeast of the house, certainly a necessity before Mrs. Sharrer could move in, but there is no record of when this was done or how much it cost.

Presumably Mrs. Sharrer occupied her house for the first time in the summer of 1897. She may well have felt the constraints of her small living space, for in the spring of 1900, she had an additional room built on to the north side of the house. But she did not live long to enjoy Jamestown summers in her own home. She died a year later. She was only forty-seven.

Her children inherited the property, and unlike her parents, daughter Josephine lived to the fine age of eighty-four. She had three children, and in 1929, she and her husband bought another house on an adjoining lot so their children could bring their families to enjoy Jamestown summers. Thus the portable house, no longer portable, became with the passing years the nucleus for summer gatherings for Jeannette Sharrer's children, grandchildren, great-grandchildren, and great-great-grandchildren.

The 1895 Ducker catalogue urges prospective purchasers "to note that though the buildings are apparently of light construction, and can be erected with great facility, they are not of frail construction, and therefore liable to be affected by exposure or subject to risks from severe storms." Ducker Portable House Style No. 14 certainly testified to the validity of that promise. It survived the Hurricane of 1938 and Hurricane Carol in 1954. Not until the early 1970s was it finally pulled down to make a place for a newer and larger house, also a prefab.

It cost almost as much to dismantle the old house as it had cost to bring it to Jamestown: nearly $500.

Chapter 10
Clingstone
The House on the Rock

Joseph S.L. Wharton's Clingstone, perhaps better known as the "House on the Rock," has been described as "surely Jamestown's most unique and widely publicized abode." Wharton built Clingstone to replace Braecleugh, the handsome cottage that his father, Charles Wharton, had built on the south shore of the Dumplings peninsula in 1883. The military had taken Braecleugh when Fort Wetherill was built at the beginning of the twentieth century, and Wharton chose the unusual site for his new summer home in part to thwart any future military interest in his property.

To design his house, Wharton enlisted the help of Philadelphia artist William Trost Richards, who had also lost his summer home, Greycliff, to the Fort Wetherill expansion, and John Dixon Johnston, a Newport architect/builder. Together they designed a three-story house with twenty-three rooms, each with views of the bay from at least two sides.

Architecturally, the house defies easy categorization. Shingle style was the prevalent architectural mode in Jamestown, and Clingstone has many of the irregularities characteristic of the style, as well as cedar shingles both inside and out. The shallow-pitched roof with overhangs and shed dormers, however, hint at the newly popular bungalow style.

Johnston was probably responsible for the house's sturdy construction. Rock for the foundation and lower walls was blasted from the island itself. Solid oak beams and heavy mill-type framing covered by diagonal sheathing were designed to withstand hurricane-force winds. The interior cladding of shingles was practical both because of the dampness that invaded the

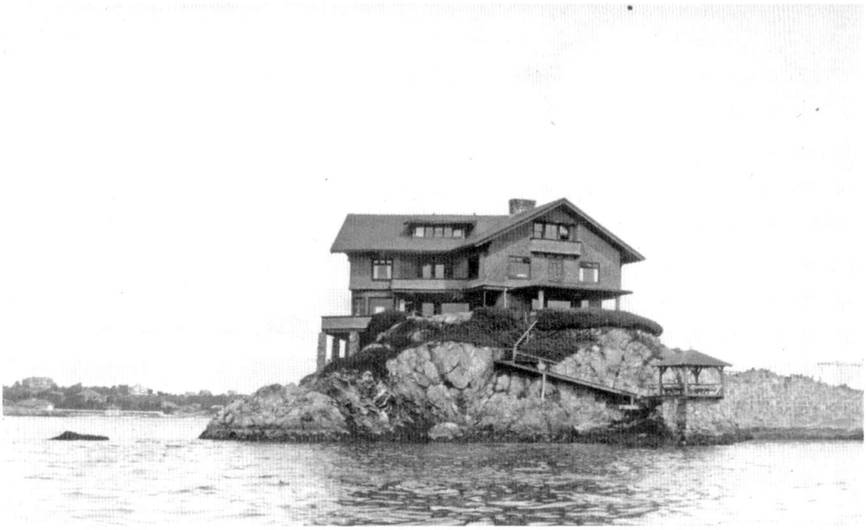

Clingstone, the Whartons' summer cottage built in 1904–05. The summerhouse in the foreground has long since disappeared. *Jamestown Historical Society, Henry Wood Collection (P2008.014.020).*

unheated house in the winter and because Fort Wetherill's cannons went off so regularly in training exercises that they cracked the plaster in the neighboring houses. The rest of the interior is equally rugged, with massive beachstone fireplaces and burlap-covered ceilings.

Completed in 1905, the Whartons' new cottage was entirely self-sufficient. A vast cistern held rainwater that was collected throughout the year, and a diesel engine pumped the water through the house and provided electricity. The family's growing fleet was moored in a nearby cove on Conanicut Island. (The facilities there later became the Wharton Shipyard and are now the Jamestown Boat Yard.) An underwater telephone cable connected the cottage to the captain's house at the shipyard, and the captain stood ready to provide transportation to and from the cottage.

Most people think that the house's name describes its unusual construction, clinging to a rock jutting out of the bay. According to the family, the name is a pun. Soon after it was completed, a friend remarked to Wharton "it is a peach of a house." The double meaning appealed to Wharton, who named the house after the clingstone peach as well as the site.

Clingstone was ideal for a family who loved the sea and boating. The Wharton boys, at an early age, were given free rein to sail anywhere in the bay as long as they could see Clingstone. Boaters of all ages continue to rely on this unique summer cottage as an aid to navigation.

The Whartons summered at Clingstone until the late 1930s, and the house stood empty for the next two decades. It remained structurally sound through the Hurricane of 1938, which washed away the stone pier, and Hurricane Carol in 1954, although it suffered greatly from the wind that broke the windows and the water that blew through the house. Vandals, too, took their toll. Generations of teenagers used the old empty house for parties, burning furniture and loose pieces of wood in the fireplaces and leaving behind other evidence of their escapades. Interior shingles on the second floor are embedded with marbles that had been blasted there by some sort of firearm.

In 1961, Henry Wood, an architect cousin of the Whartons, bought Clingstone for $3,600—the price of the back taxes—and started a long program of restoration. Today, the house is totally "green." A wind turbine on the roof generates electricity. Solar panels heat water for household use, and photovoltaic cells charge a bank of batteries in the basement. Rainwater is collected in a three-thousand-gallon cistern and then filtered, treated, and pumped through the house for cleaning purposes. Composting toilets use only a quart of water per flush; the compost is then used to fertilize the garden. There are also waterless urinals.

Over the years, this fine old cottage has been the subject of many newspaper articles and anecdotes—some accurate, some not. The most persistent story tells of a tennis court that was washed away in the Hurricane of 1938. There were even some who "remembered" playing tennis there. According to the family, no tennis court existed. The only other structure was a teahouse that sat on a small "dumpling" next to the house. A boardwalk connected the two buildings. The teahouse was destroyed in the Hurricane of 1938.

Chapter 11

The Rise and Fall of Conanicut Park

On October 7, 1872, the John J. Watson and Hopkins farms at the North End were auctioned. The 160 acres were bought by Lucius C. Davis, the editor of the *Newport Daily News*, for $10,020. He soon sold them to the Conanicut Land Company. The purchase was the first step in the development of "a new watering place" on Narragansett Bay. Three months and about $42,600 later, the company controlled an area that extended from the East Passage to the West Passage from the northern tip of the island south almost to what is now America Way.

The Conanicut Land Company was definitely *not* a Jamestown venture. None of the four men who spearheaded it—Davis, Henry Lippitt, John Kendrick, and Leonard Whitney Jr.—had ever lived on the island. Only Davis lived in southern Rhode Island, and he used his paper to get out the word about the new community envisioned by the Conanicut Land Company investors. He wrote that the land company proposed to "make extensive improvements in the way of building a wharf, laying out streets, erecting a hotel, and otherwise fitting the section for summer residences."

Jamestown passed its first zoning code in 1935, only about twenty years after New York City's first comprehensive code of 1916. But in the nineteenth century, the town had no laws about lot size, building use, setbacks, or any of the other things that establish the look and feel of a neighborhood. The company divided the farms into two thousand house lots, many as small as five thousand square feet—about two-thirds the size of the smallest buildable lot in the village today.

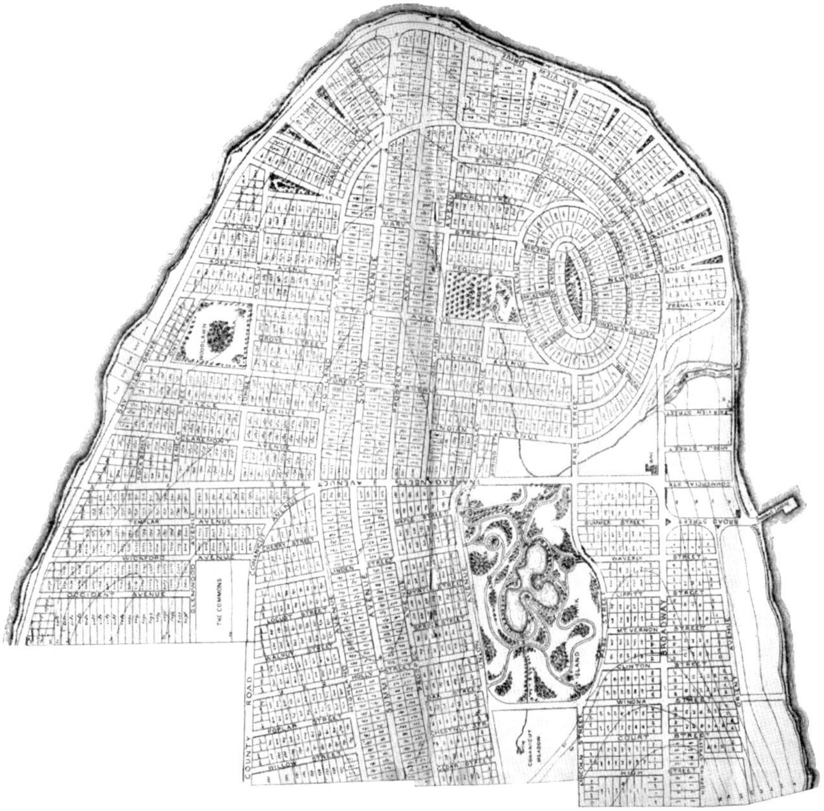

Plat map for Conanicut Park. *Jamestown Historical Society (A2006.348.001).*

To make the tiny lots more attractive, some were laid out around a common and fitted into a curving pattern of roads that followed the contour of the land and shoreline. An orchard, woodlands, and a park with curving paths were designed to give the inland cottages a more open feel.

A wharf at Broad Street could accommodate the large Providence–Newport steamships, ensuring that people from Providence and beyond could reach the resort easily. A delightfully Victorian waiting room for ferry passengers stood at the end of the wharf with a bathing house nearby. The Conanicut Park Hotel looked east from a rise just north of the long ferry wharf.

What the plans did not include were improvement of roads to the small village at East Ferry or ferry connectivity with the southern part of the island. While politically part of the town of Jamestown, Conanicut Park would be effectively a separate village, occupied only in the summer.

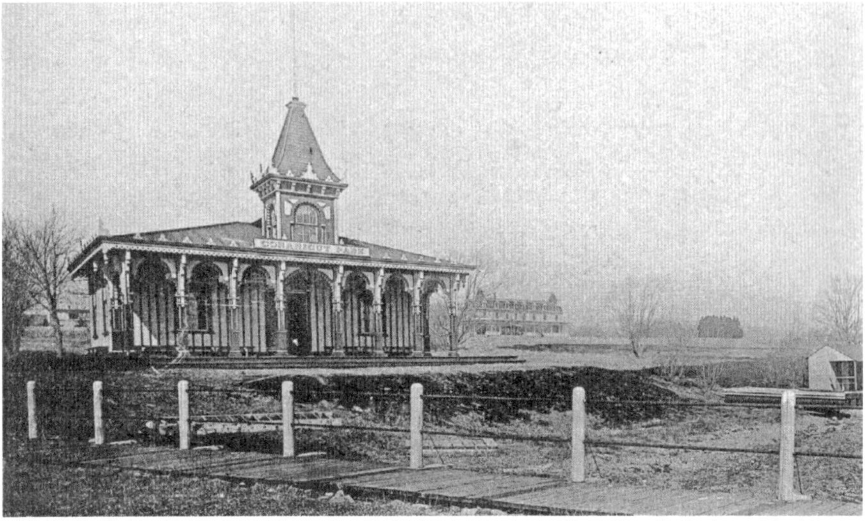

The waiting room on the wharf at Conanicut Park with the Conanicut Park Hotel in the background. *Jamestown Historical Society (A2006.168.001).*

When the small hotel—expanded two years later to accommodate about one hundred guests—opened in 1874, it was fully booked. At two dollars a day for seasonal visitors and three dollars a day for day trippers, the prices were low enough that, as one newspaper reported in 1876, "even the poorest of us may take a rest during the dog days."

Each year, newspapers reported new amenities for the visitors. Attractions at the hotel included boating, bathing, a livery stable, and a bowling alley. In the evenings, guest speakers lectured on varied subjects, and musicians played for dancing and singing. Magicians and ventriloquists entertained the children. Clergy from different faiths conducted Sunday morning services.

By 1876, so many steamers put in at the wharf that men could commute daily to their businesses in Providence. Roads were improved. A benefit festival in 1882 attracted five hundred people and realized $700 for Seaside Home, the forerunner of the YWCA Camp Seaside established in 1877 for women who worked in factories in nearby cities. The Conanicut Park developers were among the directors of the Conanicut Telegraph and Telephone Company, which made the first attempt to bring telephone service to Jamestown in 1883. A non-denominational chapel was added to the complex in 1886.

Most of the visitors stayed at the hotel, but some small Victorian cottages with gingerbread trim and deep porches were available. One cottage on Hillside Avenue—now the upper reaches of East Shore Road—was advertised for sale in 1874 for $2,500.

Although the hotel was a success, land sales lagged. About half of the land platted for Conanicut Park remained in the hands of the Conanicut Land Company. Many of those who bought lots purchased more than one, perhaps because of the small size of the lots. Only about forty cottages were built, and most of these were on the streets close to the hotel and wharf.

Among the earliest cottages built was Stonewall Cottage at 1026 East Shore Road. The house, distinguished by its exuberant Victorian detail and two-and-a-half-story square tower with mansard roof, was built in 1873 for Jeanie Lippitt, the daughter of Henry Lippitt, a textile magnate and first president of the Conanicut Land Company. Lippitt was governor of Rhode Island from 1874 to 1876 and was largely responsible for the establishment in 1876 of the Providence Day School for the Deaf, now the Rhode Island School for the Deaf. He had a personal interest in teaching the deaf. Jeanie Lippitt had lost her hearing after contracting scarlet fever when she was four, and her mother had taught her to read lips and to speak.

Twelve years later, Charles Fletcher built his impressive Conanicut Park cottage with its asymmetrical octagonal tower nearby at 1076 East Shore Road. Fletcher came to Rhode Island from England in the late 1860s and built an empire for the production of woolen cloth. By the early 1880s, he employed three thousand workers in nine mills. In 1886, he came to Jamestown and turned part of his energy to becoming an accomplished yachtsman. He added a wing to the house for his daughter Jane's wedding in 1896.

Throughout the 1870s and into the 1880s, the new resort prospered. But in mid-July 1887, disaster struck the Conanicut Park Hotel. An illness that, according to the *Newport Daily News*, resembled "old-fashioned dysentery with cramps in the neck and back," first hit on July 17. Soon, everyone staying at the hotel was affected, but none of the cottagers, even those close to the hotel, were afflicted.

At first, no one had a clue what the illness was or its cause. A doctor who had treated some of the patients opined that outbreaks such as this were probably not caused by water but were aerial, but he hedged, saying that such illnesses could indeed be introduced by impure water. Whatever the cause, all the hotel guests left. Expected visitors were advised by telegraph and mail to cancel their plans.

Water from a well that was used for drinking and cooking was sent to Brown University. Analysis showed no contamination, and the water was

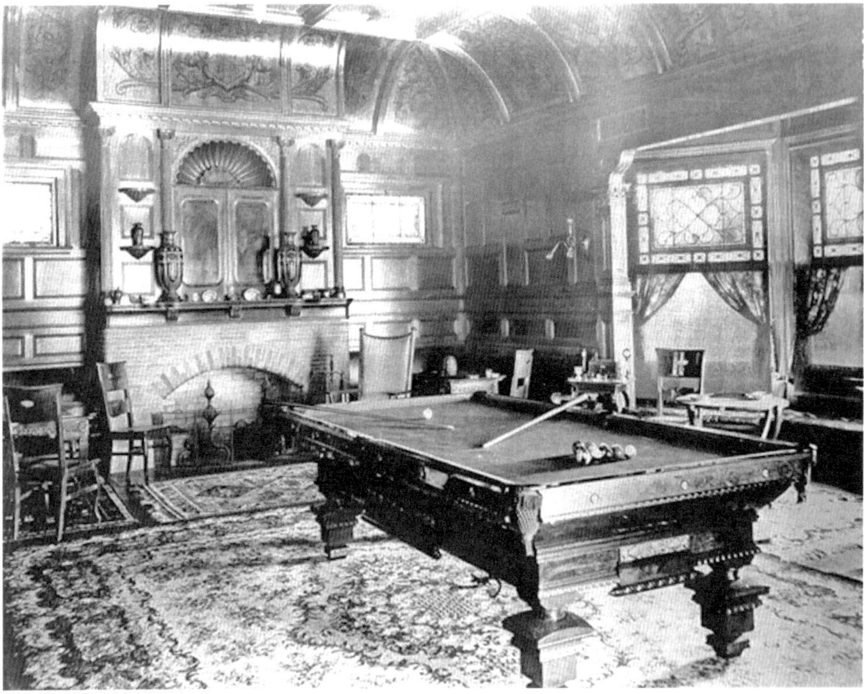

Billiard room at the Fletcher cottage in Conanicut Park. Charles Fletcher added the room for his daughter Jane Elizabeth's wedding in 1896. *Jamestown Historical Society (P1998.002).*

certified as fit for domestic use. Next, the ice in use in the hotel, which was brought over from Newport, was analyzed and declared pure.

The *New York Times* carried a story about the illness on July 25. Two days after its initial story, the *Times* reported that Dr. W. Argyle Watson, a summer Jamestowner from New York, had found the cause of the epidemic. Sewer pipes from water closets in the hotel joined the main sewer under the laundry room in the hotel basement. Nearby was an old well. Water from this secondary well was used only for flushing toilets in the upper stories of the hotel. The laundry room flooring was removed, exposing a broken sewer line and a mass of reeking, filthy sewage running into the old well. A bad odor had been detected coming from the well several days before the discovery, and a pump had been placed in the new well. But the damage had already been done.

The immediate problem was solved by changing the source of all water used in the hotel. Water from cisterns and from a nearby brook, which provided water described as having the highest and purest character, was pumped through new iron pipes with leaded joints. The hotel reopened for the remainder of the season on July 29. Prospective guests were told that the plumbing had been put in most perfect condition. How many guests returned that summer is unknown.

Meanwhile, all the dirt in the vicinity of the broken pipe joint was removed. The old well was filled up. The newer well was also filled, even though it was some fifty feet away from the problem site.

The 1888 season began well, the scare of the preceding summer seemingly forgotten. Newspaper ads stated: "New and complete plumbing. Drainage perfect. Not a cesspool or well on the premises. Running spring water introduced from a distance." The hotel had more guests than at any previous time.

A new road from the East Ferry to Conanicut Park along the east shore brought day visitors from Newport to the hotel for afternoon tea. Summer activities went on at the usual pace—trips to Beavertail and Newport, services at the little chapel every Sunday, and the second-annual tennis tournament with "spirited play and prizes fairly earned by the excellent playing of the winners." In September, the Conanicut Park Improvement Society held its annual meeting. Committees were appointed on transportation, streets, and walks. Hearty agreement was expressed on the hopeful outlook for the Park.

The prosperity was superficial. Most of the platted lots remained unsold. The Conanicut Land Company owed two mortgages totaling $23,000. The activity at the hotel could not sustain the development.

In October 1889, the *Providence Journal* advertised the sale at auction of Conanicut Park, "a Most Beautiful and Desirable Summer Resort on Narragansett Bay, within thirty minutes sail of Newport and an easy access from New York, Boston and Providence," with four hundred acres of land platted into house lots, a first-class hotel with all furnishings, two good cottages, a large public wharf with a passenger station adjoining, bathhouses and bowling alley. The offering was for the completely listed property, subject to mortgages that would be assumed by the purchaser.

Former governor Henry Lippitt, one of the original investors, purchased the property for $12,000. He sold some individual lots and leased out the hotel for several years, but he, too, was soon trying to unload the property. Neither he nor members of his family had the time or interest to run a resort.

The new century saw the end of Conanicut Park. The hotel did not open for the 1900 summer season. Although some families still summered in the cottages they had built in the area's heyday, other cottages were rented to the YWCA, which had established Camp Seaside for young workingwomen nearby.

For a while, the Conanicut Park Improvement Society operated a casino—a gathering place for the cottagers—on the first floor of the hotel. In 1906, Rhode Island Hospital leased the property for convalescing children who, it was felt, would benefit from the "attractive outdoor life" on the island.

In early 1909, after ten years of only sporadic use, the building was torn down. That September, the *Providence Journal* carried a large advertisement for the auction of the Conanicut Park plat, "450 acres of land on Narragansett Bay with more than two miles of shore front." The property was to be auctioned in two parcels. Parcel number one, about 385 acres, contained 1,579 building lots, most of them fifty by one hundred feet, with streets, parks, and unplatted land, along with riparian rights, water system, waiting station, and two houses. Parcel number two, which included a farm of about 67 acres, adjoined parcel number one on the south.

The Lippitt family heirs had ordered the sale. The final sale price for the 450 acres was $11,000—only $80 more than Lucius Davis had paid for just 160 acres thirty-seven years earlier.

Chapter 12

Building Jamestown Shores

The development of Jamestown Shores, the largest single subdivision in Jamestown, began in late 1946 when the Federal Building and Development Corporation, a private development group, purchased the Tefft, Gladding, and Maxfield farms. The farms extended for almost two miles north along the west shore from just south of the six-year-old Jamestown Bridge. The adjacent Hammond farm was added in August 1947.

The first four Jamestown Shores plats were recorded on March 22 and April 24, 1947. On April 28—the Monday after the fourth plat was recorded—the Jamestown Town Council established the planning commission to oversee subdivision development.

From the beginning, the vision of the development corporation, led by James G. Head (a newcomer to the island and not one of the Jamestown Heads who had lived on the island since the nineteenth century), differed from that of the new planning commission.

Head envisioned a seaside community of small summer cottages. The majority of the lots in the original plats were 7,200 square feet, and deeds required a minimum house size of 576 square feet. Three weeks after the plats were recorded, on May 17, the commission issued the first "Rules and Regulations Governing and Restricting the Platting or Other Subdivision of Land." The rules set the minimum size of a subdivision lot at 10,000 square feet.

The subdivision design included roads with boating names like Frigate and Garboard. Lot owners were granted an easement to use eight developer-

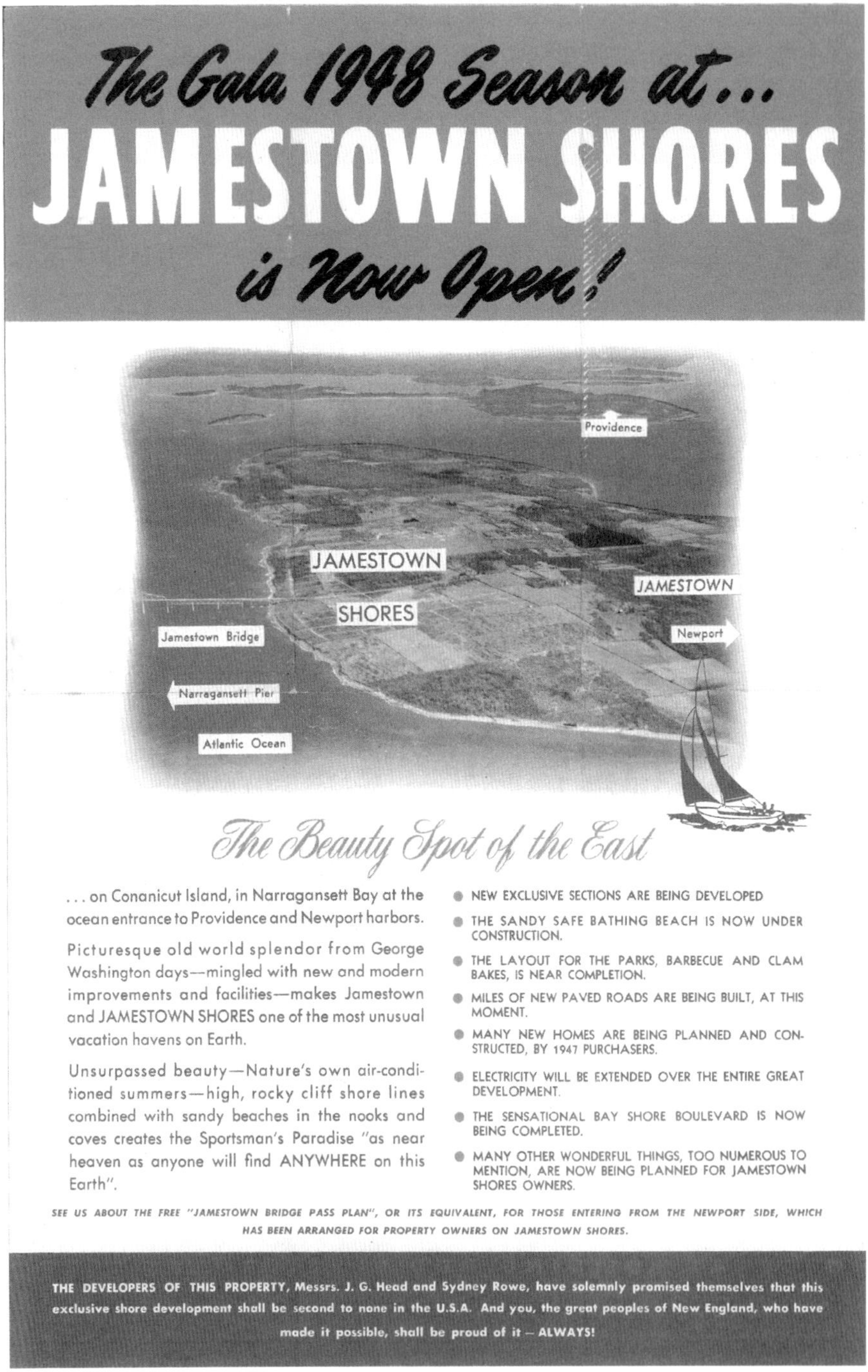

Sales poster for Jamestown Shores in 1948. *Jamestown Historical Society (P2004M.411).*

owned shore lots "and waters adjacent thereto for the purpose of bathing and swimming." The developers made no provision for water, sewer, telephone, electricity or other form of power, or police and fire protection.

The first lot was sold on May 27, 1947, and within three years, 110 families had built homes in the area. Almost all of the early houses were summer homes, most often for people from central Massachusetts or northern Rhode Island, who in the years before the interstate preferred a two-hour ride to Jamestown to the six-hour grind to Cape Cod. As time passed and transportation to and from the island improved, the original cottages were enlarged and converted to year-round residences, although many were still occupied only part of the year.

Head promised the planning commission that Eldred Avenue, which ran from the Jamestown Bridge across the island to East Shore Road, would be the only business artery in the Shores. Business lots would be no smaller than 7,200 square feet, and he would keep the area free of "cheap and unsightly structures." The Jamestown Shores Motel and a small restaurant—known in the 1980s as Mr. Pipes—on the north side of Eldred Avenue at the foot of the bridge were the only commercial buildings erected. They were torn down in the mid-1980s to make way for the new Jamestown Verrazzano Bridge and the John Eldred Parkway.

Isolated from the village by the surrounding farms and the marsh, usually with no family links to the island, and essentially deserted by the developer who moved to Florida, Jamestown Shores residents created their own tightly knit community.

Electricity came to the area through the action of a Jamestown Shores resident, Armand Girard, who in 1949 contracted with the Newport Electric Co. to pay $1 per month per pole for each pole on North Main Road between Eldred Avenue and Frigate Street—a cost of $35 per month, or over $300 a month in today's dollars. As customers subscribed to the service, the cost was divided among them until enough homes were electrified to allow metering.

In 1950, forty-six families formed the Jamestown Shores Association to promote the welfare of the area in "an atmosphere of neighborliness and friendship." The association began to address—one by one—the problems these families faced because of their isolation and the short-sightedness of the original development.

The roads in the development had been deeded to the town shortly after the project opened. Legally, however, the town had no obligation to repair or improve them. The association brought political pressure to include the roads in the town budget.

The community beach belonged to the developers, who initially landscaped the area, installed picnic tables and grills, and designated parking areas but did not maintain these amenities. The association arranged a lease in 1955. The town later bought the beach, and it is now open to all Jamestowners with resident stickers.

Feeling that the Jamestown Police Department did not have a high enough presence in the dense residential area of the Shores, the association's Ellen Conroy introduced the first crime watch program in Jamestown. The group later helped to introduce crime watch to other parts of the island.

The association and Jamestown Shores' residents in general were especially active during the planning for the Jamestown Verrazzano Bridge and the John Eldred Parkway in the 1980s and early 1990s. The new limited access highway followed the old Eldred Avenue route and passed directly through the development, further limiting communication between the northern and southern sections. Because the only fire station is in the village, the people in the Shores were particularly concerned that fire equipment would be able to reach all parts of the area easily.

The association remains a political and social advocate for the area, sponsoring "meet the candidate" nights and speaking out on issues that particularly affect the local residents.

Water and wastewater disposal continue to be major concerns in Jamestown Shores. Each of the over eight hundred developed lots has its own septic system and well, and both town and state regulations aimed at avoiding cross-contamination have become increasingly stringent. The area is also subject to the high ground water table ordinance, which restricts construction that could limit the ability of rainfall and treated wastewater to replenish drinking water supplies or that could encourage salt water intrusion.

Part III
Getting Here

Chapter 13

A Stop on the Steamship Route Between New York and Fall River

That Jamestown should ever boast of a direct line to New York probably never occurred to any of the residents of Newport's sister resort across the bay until there were rumors last winter…Now there are daily sailings and landings of a line of Sound steamers in opposition to the long established Fall River Line.
—Newport Journal, *June 30, 1906*

At the beginning of the twentieth century, despite its growing reputation as a summer resort, Jamestown remained isolated from the rest of the state. Only the Jamestown & Newport Ferry Company—partially owned by the town and governed by a board of directors elected by the people of Jamestown—provided transport to and from the town. The traffic up and down the bay bypassed the island.

The New York, New Haven, and Hartford Railroad had a virtual monopoly on both passenger and freight traffic between Boston and Philadelphia. The luxurious boats of the railroad's subsidiary Fall River Line carried travelers overnight between New York City and Newport and on to Fall River, where they could make train connection to Boston. The trip was much more comfortable than traveling by road—which, before the advent of the automobile, were mostly unpaved—or even by the railroad itself since several changes were needed to cross unbridged rivers or to transfer from one line to another.

The turn of the century brought serious competition to the Fall River Line—and with it an opportunity for Jamestown and the Jamestown &

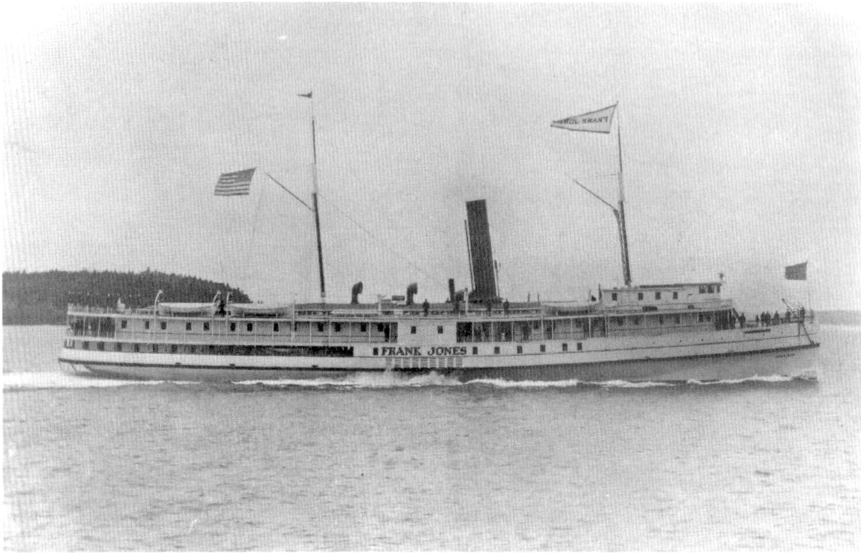

The *Frank Jones*, the flagship of the Enterprise Line. *Courtesy of Joe Bains.*

Newport Ferry Company. David Whitcomb founded the Enterprise Line in 1904, and on June 1, 1905, the Enterprise Line's *Frank Jones*—also the name of a popular New England beer—made its initial passenger run from Fall River to New York City. Neither as new nor as large as the Fall River Line steamers, the ship offered both convenience and lower prices. It left New York and Fall River on alternate nights. The Enterprise Line pier in Fall River was convenient to the trolley line to Providence. Advertisements promoted the line's one-dollar passenger fare for the overnight trip and a twenty-cent trolley ride into the city.

The following month, the *Warren*—188 feet long and built in 1874—began carrying freight on a similar schedule. That summer, the *Newport Mercury* reported that about one quarter of Newport's fishing business had gone to Fall River to take advantage of the Enterprise's lower shipping rates. In September, the *Kennebec* joined the *Frank Jones*, and passenger service was expanded to six days a week.

The Fall River Line was clearly feeling the impact of the competing line. When the Enterprise Line tried to expand its service to Newport, its attempts to obtain a suitable place to land were blocked.

The Jamestown & Newport Ferry Company offered an alternative. In January 1906, the two companies reached an agreement. Under the terms of the contract, the ferry company promised to erect a suitable landing before May 1, 1906. The Enterprise Line agreed to lease the landing site for ten years, with the privilege of renewal for ten more years, and to pay the ferry company the cost of the pier extension in lieu of lease payments for the first ten years. All Enterprise Line steamers would stop at Jamestown starting on April 1. The ferry company would "transport on a proper and convenient schedule, between Jamestown and Newport," all passengers and goods coming to or from the steamers and would serve as the sole agent of the Enterprise Line for the transaction of business in Jamestown. In return, the Enterprise Line gave the ferry company a commission on all Enterprise Line tickets it sold and paid the ferry company a percentage of its gross receipts for freight.

On May 1, 1906, a large crowd—estimated to be the largest non-summer crowd for any Conanicut Island event—assembled on the new dock to greet the *Frank Jones* when it stopped for the first time on its way to New York City. The Jamestown Brass Band played before the ship arrived at 8:00 p.m. and after it left at 8:20 p.m., carrying a load of passengers and fish. The next morning, the *Kennebec* landed on its way to Fall River.

The new service was a success. As promised, the Jamestown & Newport Ferry Company provided timely connections for Newport passengers. On June 2, the *Newport Journal* announced that 191 passengers had ridden the ferry from Newport to Jamestown on the previous Friday, over half bound

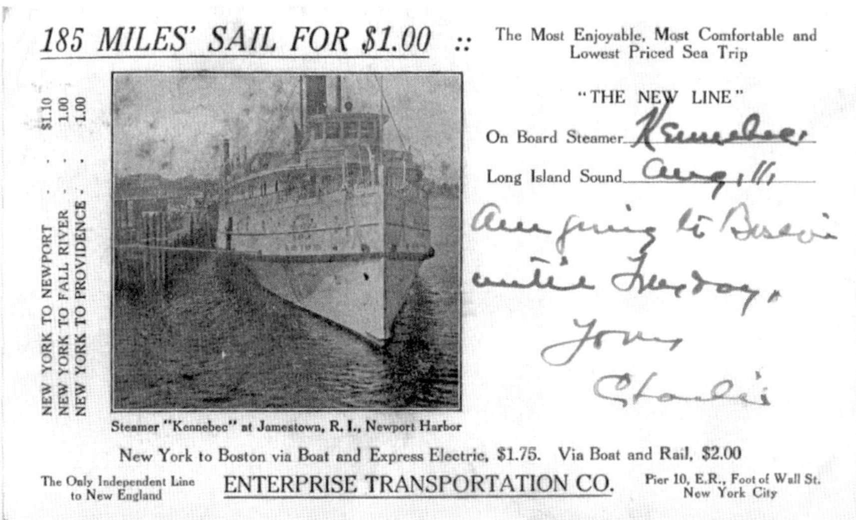

The *Kennebec* at the dock at East Ferry. Postcards were distributed to passengers on the steamers. *Courtesy of Joe Bains.*

for New York via the Enterprise Line. Two months after the first landing, the *Journal* reported, "On one landing there were 12 tons of freight for Newport alone. The summer people for Jamestown have seen the convenience of shipping their freight that way and some of the people themselves have come by the line. The steamers are not so large as some that travel the Sound, but they have made their sailings according to schedule and the patrons speak well of the accommodations given them."

The success encouraged the Jamestown & Newport Ferry Company to upgrade its facilities. A dock that projected three hundred feet out from the old wharf and had a liberal L at the head was built as a landing space for the big steamers. A gasoline streetlight was placed at the head of the wharf, and lights were put along the wharf to make it safer on dark nights. A nearby building became a comfortable waiting room. The company replaced the old freight house with a newer, larger, and more accessible one and improved the dock in Newport.

In November 1906, the Enterprise Line added a Sunday passenger sailing to New York on its newly acquired *St. Croix*. This meant a steamer was stopping at the island every day of the week.

The Enterprise Line's thriving business was not without problems. In late October, an accident involving a gasoline light in the freight house at Jamestown caused a fire that fortunately was seen by William H. Brooks and Abbott Chandler, who were in the ferry company's freight house. They ran down the wharf, beat out the fire on the floor, and, climbing up on a sawhorse, were able to extinguish the small fire in the peak of the building.

About this time, William Young of Fall River sued the Enterprise Line for $500 for breach of contract. He claimed he had bought a ticket from Fall River to Jamestown, but when he tried to leave the boat in Jamestown, the crowd boarding on the gangplank kept him from disembarking. The officer refused to put the gangplank out again, and Young was forced to go on to New York.

Early in 1907, the *Newport Journal* reported that despite the lack of work in Jamestown, only two men could be found to help unload the freight from the *Warren* at sixty cents an hour. However, the *Warren* soon experienced a more serious problem. On Saturday, February 2, 1907, it left Fall River at 10:30 p.m. in an extremely thick fog with a heavy load of freight. It had waited past its sailing time anticipating an improvement in weather, but as none came, it set off for New York. South of Rose Island, the *Warren* was forced to give way to a tow of barges, which threw it off course. That and the fog resulted in the ship running its prow up on a rock in the Dumplings just north of Clingstone. Captain Brown sounded four blasts, the distress signal. The lifeboat from the ferry *Beaver Tail* was the first to respond, followed by three tugs from Newport. The tugs made an attempt to haul the ship off the rock but failed. Through the night and the next day, men worked at removing freight to the Enterprise Company's dock at Jamestown.

A shift of wind to the northeast on Monday led to the highest tide since the ship had gone aground, and at 11:30 a.m., the tugs were able to pull the *Warren* off the rocks. Although the ship incurred damage that kept it off the line for several weeks, people judged that the Enterprise Line was lucky in freeing it when and as easily as they did. The *Journal* expressed the opinion that the *Warren*'s hull, built of wood before that material became scarce, stood it in good stead, as a steel vessel would have been in more serious difficulty.

Schedules could not always be met. In March 1907, the *Kennebec* didn't arrive until 10:30 p.m. due to an unusually heavy load of freight. A week later, it was almost twenty-four hours behind schedule, detained by heavy ice in Long Island Sound. In November, loading freight detained the *Kennebec*; in fact, it had to leave some behind because of lack of space.

Still, the Enterprise Line steamers continued to carry passengers and cargo through the spring and summer of 1907. Passengers had three choices in traveling by steamer from Fall River to New York: leave on the Enterprise Line at 6:30 p.m. for a one-dollar fare, leave at 7:00 p.m. on the Neptune Line for one dollar, or leave at 7:40 p.m. on the Fall River Line for three dollars. All the lines advertised that orchestras would be on board the ships. The Enterprise Line evidently received a profitable share of this business, for plans were developed to build two new steel-hulled boats.

Behind the scenes, a larger financial battle was being waged. The New York, New Haven, and Hartford Railroad, the parent company of the Fall River Line, acquired the Joy Line, its only other major competitor in Narragansett Bay, in December 1905. Using Joy Line assets, it created the low-cost Neptune Line to compete with the Enterprise Line, especially for the freight business.

The link between the shipping and railroad interests led to an appeal to the Interstate Commerce Commission in 1907. The Enterprise Line accused the New Haven and the Pennsylvania railroads of pricing policies designed to limit access to the Pennsylvania market. Specifically, it alleged that the Pennsylvania Railroad charged almost twice as much to tranship fish from New York to Philadelphia when the fish was brought from Jamestown on an Enterprise Line ship as when the fish was shipped from Newport on a ship owned by a New York, New Haven, and Hartford Railroad subsidiary.

Although the Enterprise's shipping rates to New York were considerably less than its competitors', the total cost of the fish when it reached Philadelphia was over 10 percent higher. In the complaint, Enterprise stated that it had shipped some six thousand barrels of fish from Jamestown, and it was the only reasonable and satisfactory service from Jamestown.

An Interstate Commerce Commission hearing was held in July, and the Enterprise Line won its case: "It [the Pennsylvania Railroad] should, in our opinion, establish a joint through rate which should not exceed from Jamestown to Philadelphia 34 cents per 100 pounds, and it should receive of that rate a reasonable portion for its service."

It was a hollow victory. The financial panic of October 1907 proved too much for the "only dependable steamship line on Long Island Sound." On the evening of Friday, November 14, the *Kennebec* sailed from Fall River for the last time. The Enterprise Line went into receivership. The Jamestown & Newport Ferry Company was listed as one of the many creditors, with $722.86 owed to it.

Roger W. McAdam in his book *Floating Palaces* comments of the Enterprise Line, "It is probably the only line they [New Haven Railroad] did not have to buy at the line's own price to get rid of it."

Chapter 14

Bridges and the Course of History

Bridges, or Lack of Them, Have Determined the Course of History," proclaimed a *Wickford Standard* headline in 1937 during the acrimonious debate about whether to build a bridge to Jamestown across the West Passage. Bridge proponents won. The Jamestown Bridge opened in July 1940.

Despite the dire prophecies of its opponents, the bridge did not attract "kidnappers, beggars, marauding thieves, a class of picnickers, hot dog stands and other undesirables." The anticipated crime wave did not take place. Instead, the quiet, rural town where the pace had quickened slightly during the summer months slowly transitioned into a predominantly bedroom community for urban centers on the mainland and Aquidneck Island.

As early as April 21, 1940, three months before the bridge opened, the *New York Times* quoted a local realtor as saying, "A noticeable upturn in real estate activity has taken place since work started on the [Jamestown] bridge. Considerable acreage is available on the island for development with small homes of the Cape Cod type on quarter and half acre lots and several builders from New York and Boston are now looking over the properties."

When the bridge opened, the tolls to cross it were high. Cars cost $0.90 one way or $1.60 round trip. For comparison, dinner at Tefft's restaurant at East Ferry was recorded on a bridge commissioner's expense account at $1.10. Some—but not many—volume discounts were negotiated. In one instance, the developers of Jamestown Shores, the first major development after the bridge was built, got a volume discount for potential buyers—and incidentally potential bridge users—that reduced the one-way toll to $0.25 as a premium for looking at the land.

For fourteen years, the Jamestown Bridge Commission, a private corporation that had raised the funds to build the bridge without state help and owed $1,808,000.00 when the bridge opened, held the line on tolls, despite considerable pressure to reduce them. After 1954, the tolls were slowly reduced until in 1968 a car could cross the bridge for $0.25. The toll went back up to $0.35 the following year.

The high-priced bridge with its scary openwork grill roadway on the center span changed Jamestown from an island to, as one proponent phrased it, an "artificial peninsula." The people of Jamestown adapted to the changes gradually. At first, people continued to look to Newport. A passenger ticket for the ferry cost much less than the bridge toll. Newport shops were familiar and close to the wharf. Until well after World War II, few people had cars or, until rationing was lifted, gas. High school students still took the ferry to school on Aquidneck Island.

For born islanders, the bridge made the mainland accessible although not necessarily attractive. "The bridge got us out. We were almost tied in here," remarked one resident. But, as another commented, "there was nowhere to go anyway."

Businesses found the bridge useful. E.B. Brooks Fuel Company could deliver gasoline by tanker truck across the bridge. The E.R. Vieira Company no longer had to go to Providence via the ferry and Fall River to get coal. Smith Florists' trips to the mainland were freed from the dictates of the ferry schedule. Medical treatment in an emergency did not have to wait for a ferry.

The bridge invited newcomers. Commute time to Providence was less than one hour. Travel across southern Rhode Island between Newport and Washington Counties, both major tourist destinations, became more efficient.

Population grew by almost 10 percent in the 1950s and a startling 28 percent in the 1960s. New seasonal and year-round residents used the bridge regularly. More through travelers crossed the island, particularly in the summer. Between 1940 and 1969, the year the Newport Bridge was built, traffic on the Jamestown Bridge increased approximately 8 to 10 percent each year. In 1969, 3,200 vehicles crossed it daily. Many of these vehicles were on their way to Newport. The wait for the Jamestown & Newport Ferry could be lengthy, and the stores in the East Ferry area flourished.

Bigger changes were yet to come. The Newport Bridge (renamed the Claiborne Pell Bridge in 1992) across the East Passage opened on June 28, 1969. On the same day, the toll on the Jamestown Bridge was removed. The

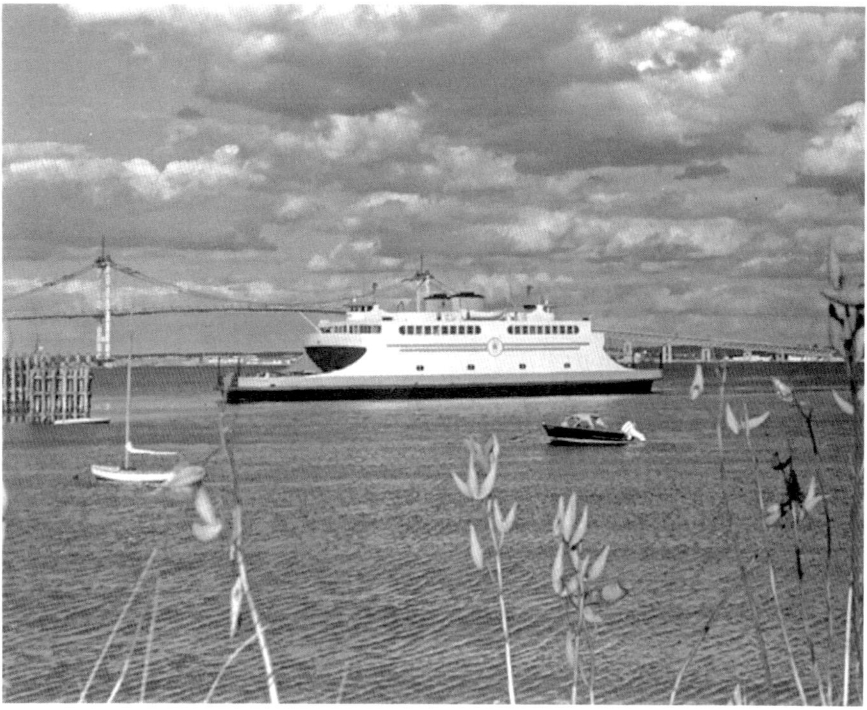

The Jamestown ferry in 1969 with the nearly completed Newport Bridge beyond. Photograph by Victor Richardson. *Jamestown Historical Society (P1973.084).*

Providence Journal noted, "The extension of Route 95 toward Jamestown and the construction of the Newport Bridge have been responsible for ending the isolation of this sleepy little island town."

Between 1970 and 1990, Jamestown's population grew 72 percent. The number of vehicles crossing the old Jamestown Bridge daily increased fifteen fold to about 20,400 vehicles—well above the number for which the fifty-year-old bridge had been designed. To accommodate the new residents, large residential subdivisions, occupying hundreds of acres, were platted north of the bridges in an area that had been relatively untouched by the early twentieth-century resort growth.

The Newport Bridge ironically increased the tendency of the local inhabitants to look to the west. With the Jamestown Bridge now toll free, going to the mainland was cheaper than going to Newport. The 1970 decision to send secondary school students to North Kingstown High School on the mainland rather than Rogers High School in Newport also helped to shift orientation westward.

For many, however, the Jamestown Bridge itself remained a barrier. Strategies for getting across the grate on the center span ranged from "put your foot on the gas and go as fast as you can" to "go slowly and steadily; just don't brake—and don't look down." Stories circulated about crumbling concrete piers. Trucks and school buses were banned from the old bridge in September 1991, and although the ban was lifted quickly, it was the last straw for many.

Travel between the two bridges was along local roads. Normally traffic from the Jamestown Bridge flowed across the island on Eldred Avenue to East Shore Road and then down East Shore Road to the Newport Bridge. On summer weekends, crossing Eldred Avenue at North Road was almost impossible.

When traffic got too backed up on the route between the bridges, drivers looked for alternate routes. They headed south on North Road and through the village, sometimes losing themselves in the warren of streets south of Shoreby Hill. In 1977, in an attempt to alleviate the congestion, the first stop-and-go traffic lights on the island were installed at the North Road and Eldred Avenue intersection. As the traffic on the island worsened, Jamestowners supported plans to replace the Jamestown Bridge and to upgrade and realign Route 138 across the island.

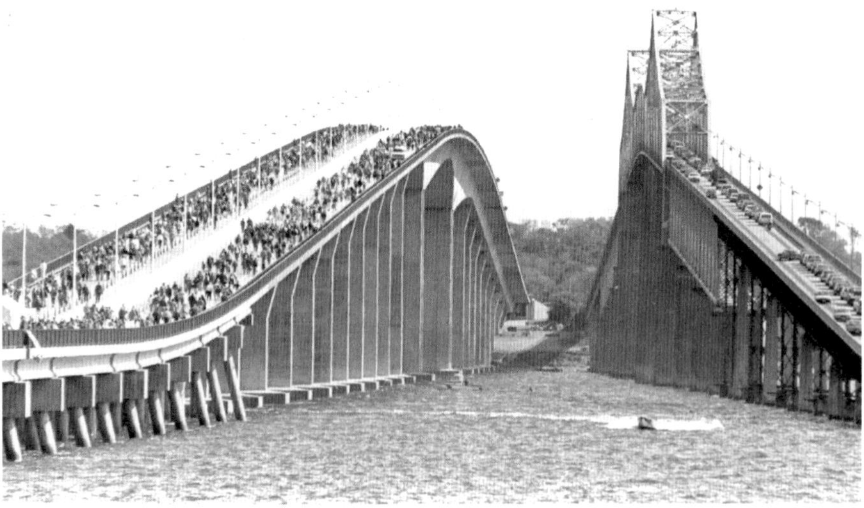

The Jamestown Verrazzano Bridge, October 17, 1992. An estimated forty thousand people walked across the span the day before the bridge opened to traffic. *Jamestown Historical Society (P2001.131)*.

Serious planning for a new bridge across the West Passage began in the mid-1970s. The initial contract for building the new bridge was awarded in December 1984. Contract disputes, changing contractors, and natural disasters delayed the construction. The new Jamestown Verrazzano Bridge across the West Passage finally opened in October 1992, $100 million over budget. The John Eldred Parkway between the two bridges was completed two years later.

With two modern bridges and an expressway connecting them, many travelers zip across Jamestown unaware that they are on an island. But others stop and stay—one thousand new residents between 1990 and 2010. Most work off-island, crossing one of the bridges each day.

On summer weekends, islanders still strategize how best to avoid the traffic snarls at the bridge exits on both sides of the bay. Or they just stay home.

Chapter 15

Old Jamestown Bridge Memories

In 2006, the year that the 1940 Jamestown Bridge was demolished, the Jamestown Historical Society and the *Jamestown Press* asked people to submit their memories of the old Jamestown Bridge. Memories came in from across the country—from Rhode Island to California to Texas. Five were chosen for publication in the *Jamestown Press*

From Chris Crawford

The Crawford family bought an abandoned house on Seaside Drive in the 1950s when it was a single-lane dirt road with six houses on its entire length. The property along the water was regularly cut down by Mr. Gladding as they were marketing the lots for $2,500 each.

It provided us seven Crawfords and a million other kids who stayed with us (my dad always volunteered for Big Brothers) a phenomenal playground on the water where we played hours of baseball, golf, football and volleyball every day as soon as we rolled out of bed. We had the equivalent of a dormitory chock full of beds, and every meal was family style. My dad refused to get a phone as we always welcomed anyone who stopped in and he could avoid calls from work.

A big part of growing up was the bridge. My dad would drive down the hill on the Saunderstown side and hit his horn, which we could clearly hear at the house—remarkable considering the volume of cars (and noise) that cross it today. We would run up to the old motel on Eldred Avenue, and then he would let one of us kids drive the car home. We always swam out and fished off the piers and once saved a jumper.

Manny Matoes one night was in the tollbooth (often quiet at night with few cars) and was watching a lightning storm and thought he saw our house, which stood out, be hit. He called the fire department, which sent out a car to check it out. Before they could even get there, he was calling them back telling of the fire that quickly mushroomed, consuming every board in the house as the department struggled to get the pumps in place from the rocky shoreline up to the house. We lost everything but never forgot his efforts to alert the fire department.

The tollbooth collectors saw everyone and knew everyone by name, as you had to buy your book of tickets from them. I am sure they were valuable eyes and ears to the police department year round and were definitely part of making Jamestown a welcoming place.

From Nancy Crawford

In late January 1981, I was bringing my daughter Kerry home after being born several days earlier at Kent Hospital in Warwick. We had an old car back then and lived in a small cottage in view of the bridge in Jamestown Shores. The car broke down just before the main span of the bridge, coming to a slow stop. It was a cold, windy day, and the bridge was deserted except for us.

As my husband frantically looked under the hood for a quick answer, a small sports car pulled up and offered to help out. It was decided that this couple would bring me to our house, and I would call a tow truck from there. Now, I am so afraid of heights that the thought of stepping onto that bridge was terrifying. What my husband failed to tell the helpful young couple was that I also had a newborn baby with me—their eyes popped out when he handed them the baby first! I had to be coaxed out of the car and into theirs.

When we arrived at our house our beloved Newfoundland "Mutley" was there to greet me; unfortunately, he was not so enthusiastic about the helpful couple. So I hobbled to the door with baby in my arms only to discover I had the wrong key! Back into the car and to the bridge where a truck had pushed the car off and into the parking lot of the old motel. Keys were exchanged, and at last we were home! When my husband arrived later, the house was dark. The baby was asleep in the "home from the hospital" bunting, and I was having a postpartum meltdown on the couch.

We have laughed about this story every time we told it since, and it was written into her [Kerry's] babybook. Three children later none had such a coming home story to tell! (PS: Kerry is grown up, works in Disaster Preparedness for the government in Washington, D.C., and does not share her mom's fear of heights.)

From Judy Garlick

When there was still a toll on the Jamestown Bridge, my father, Frank Garlick, went on a business trip in a hearse to Connecticut with Art Washburn, who had a funeral home in Jamestown. On the way back, my father rested in the back of the vehicle. On reaching the tollbooth, he sat up quickly and nearly scared the toll collector to death.

From Marion L. Galvin

For many years, I had season tickets to the "Tent" (Warwick Musical Theater) and we traveled [from Newport] each week, early via the ferry, later the Newport Bridge, to reach there.

One particular night, on our way to see Liberace, as we reached the top grate of the Jamestown Bridge, we found traffic in front of us stopped all the way down the Bridge to Saunderstown. Three black-and-white cows were coming up the bridge toward us at a good pace. State and local police were on the scene, and we had to wait until a farmer and his truck arrived to corral the errant cows back to their field. Needless to say, we were late for the show but had already seen a great one anyhow!!!

FROM KEN O'GARA

"Boys Will Be Boys...Catching a Breeze on the Jamestown Bridge"

Four teenage adventurers decided to explore the Jamestown Bridge from a different perspective. The journey began on a summer afternoon in 1976 (give or take a year). The four childhood buddies from Warwick climbed over the railing and down the ladder to the two main piers at the center of the bridge.

It was a fabulous day of feelings of youth, freedom and invulnerability. After we had our share of excitement, we climbed back over the railing and headed back toward the car. Our raptured spirits soon came to an abrupt halt as a policeman greeted us on the bridge with his car lights flashing and traffic stopped. We all climbed into his squad car and were escorted back to our vehicle, which was parked on the Jamestown side of the bridge. We were then lined up against the side of my car like men

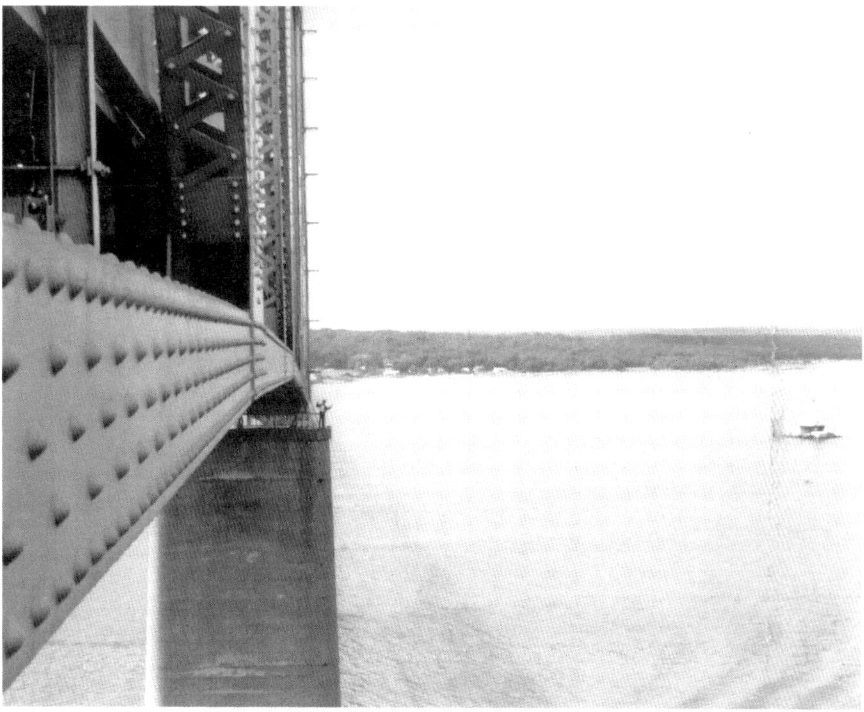

A teenager waving from the top of a concrete pier on the Jamestown Bridge. The boy is dwarfed by the pier and superstructure. *Jamestown Historical Society (P2006.016.001).*

before a firing squad. He asked us why, whose idea was it and our names, ages, addresses, phone numbers, etc.

We were told that the North Kingstown and Jamestown police departments were flooded with calls and even the Coast Guard was notified by passing pleasure craft. After the fear of God was permanently burned into our consciences, we were allowed to be on our way, wondering if we would have to answer for it again when we returned to our homes. Well, fortunately, our parents weren't notified, and all we have is this photo [on page 93] to give them a hint of how wild we were back then.

Chapter 16

The Wreck of the *Harvey F. Payton*

Thursday night we had quite a storm, and a fine large schooner came ashore near the light house. She was loaded with granite, bone dust, furniture and other things. The vessel will be a total loss. She was only three years old. They saved nearly $30,000 worth of her cargo in chronometers. I went down today to see it, everything completely ground up. Chairs. Bureaus. Sofas. Bedsteads. Cribs. Cradles. Hat trees. All kinds of Stands. And out of them all I did not see one single thing that was whole.
—letter to Thomas H. Clarke, House of Refuge, Harlem, New York, from his sister M.J. Watson, dated March 6, 1859

The *Harvey F. Payton* was a schooner, ninety-three and a half feet long with two masts. It was built in Bristol in 1855 and was owned by a group of men that included individuals from Providence, Bristol, and several towns on Cape Cod. The major investor was the Bristol shipbuilding firm of Stanton & Skinner, which owned 31 percent.

The ship was licensed for coastal trading. Its master was Asa Wheldon Nickerson from South Dennis on Cape Cod. Nickerson had captained the *Payton* since its launch in September 1855.

Not much is known about where the *Payton* traveled in the three years prior to its final voyage—its log book is lost, whether with the ship or after. If it followed the usual pattern, it traveled up and down the East Coast carrying cargo of various sorts, probably including granite on most trips.

The *Payton*'s final trip began in Boston. It had arrived in Boston from Alexandria, Virginia, on January 17. At the end of February, after forty days

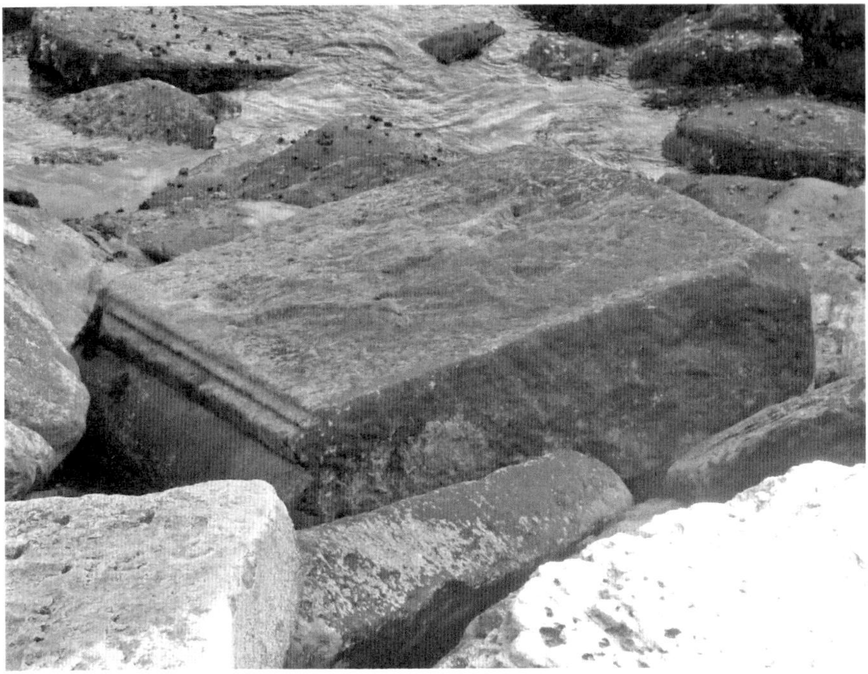

A stone from the *Harvey F. Payton*. Photograph by Michael Girard. *Jamestown Historical Society (A2014.048.001).*

in port, it set out again for Alexandria. The *Payton*'s most valuable cargo by size was twenty-two chronometers. By far the weightiest cargo was 140 tons of cut granite blocks. It also carried, according to news stories after it sank, cider, herring, bone dust, and furniture, although in what proportion is unknown.

All the large granite blocks were two feet by four feet but varied between two and eight feet in length. Some were carved with ornate fleur-de-lis. Others had edges carved with an ogee half bullnose molding. Paul J. Perkins of Wakefield, Rhode Island, researched the source of the stones and believes they came from quarries north of Boston, possibly in Chelmsford and Rockport, Massachusetts.

Perkins also investigated where the *Payton* was taking the stones. Here the evidence is unclear. Early rumors were that they were bound for Washington, D.C., to be used in the south wing of the treasury building, which was under construction from 1855 to 1861. However, Perkins uncovered records in the National Archives that confirmed that all granite for that building came from quarries in Dix Island, Maine. Other government buildings were investigated without any evidence being uncovered of delay or change due to a lost shipment. He finally concluded that the stones were probably destined for a private mausoleum. Fleur-de-lis engravings were common on structures of that kind in the mid-nineteenth century.

Late February was not a propitious time to start a sea voyage. A letter from the Boston correspondent for the *Sacramento (CA) Daily News* dated March 4, which was printed on April 1, 1859, described vividly the weather in Boston.

> *March...was ushered in by one of those driving snow storms which, for the time, suspend all out-of-door exercise for business or pleasure, and compel both man and beast to seek for shelter from the pitiless blast. During its prevalence many marine disasters occurred upon this coast, and two ships, with valuable cargoes, were lost at the entrance of our* [Boston] *harbor.*

The *Harvey F. Payton* made it out of Boston Harbor and got around the hook of Cape Cod as far as Block Island Sound before the worsening weather drove Captain Nickerson to seek refuge in Newport.

The passage into Narragansett Bay is treacherous at the best of times. Brenton Reef guards the entrance on the east. Mackerel Cove looks, from the sea, as if it were a passage between two islands. At the choke point between Fort Adams and Fort Wetherill, the East Passage narrows to about two-thirds of a mile, with rocks on either side of the deep channel.

By 1859, the Beavertail light, the third lighthouse in the British colonies, had guided sailing vessels into the bay for over a century. A "watch house" had been built at Beavertail Point sometime in the late 1600s. For over half a century, Jamestown kept the watchtower and beacon in good repair, but the navigational help it provided did not satisfy Newport ship owners. In 1749, Peter and Joseph Harrison were hired to build the first Beavertail light. The first tower, largely made of wood, was sixty-nine feet tall, with the light rising eleven feet more. The octagonal stone base was twenty-four feet in diameter, and the tower tapered to eight feet at the top of the lantern. Four years later, the light burned to the ground and was immediately replaced by a stone structure. The 1753 tower lit the entrance to the bay—with a brief hiatus during the American Revolution—until 1856.

The new Beavertail light, built in 1855–56, was sixty-four feet to the beacon. The new optic was a third-order Fresnel lens imported from France, a sparkling beehive of glass with bullseyes for focusing the beam and prisms to bend the light to the bullseyes. The light could be seen, according to a contemporary report, for fourteen miles. But not in a fog or the driving snow of March 3, 1859.

The foghorn was no more effective. The properties of sound were not clearly understood. A report from 1881 tells of a steamship that could not hear the fog signal and almost went up on the rocks at Beavertail, but "when we passed the light as closely as was safe, and abreast of it and at right angles with the direction of the wind, the fog signal broke on us suddenly and with its full power."

The *Harvey F. Payton* evidently neither saw the light nor heard the horn. Or maybe the warnings came too late. It made it into the East Passage and came to disaster on the rocks about 500 yards north of the light. According to the first newspaper report in the *Providence Journal* the next day, it was 9:00 p.m. when the ship went ashore. Later, more official, reports put the time at 8:30 p.m.

Despite the snow and the darkness of the winter night, all the crew reached shore safely. Perhaps impelled by the knowledge that the ship was uninsured and that he owned a 16 percent share, Captain Nickerson risked his life to bring sixteen of the chronometers, worth about $1,500 each, ashore. They were the only cargo salvaged from the wreck.

The ship, valued at about $10,000.00, was a total loss. The hull was sold for $112.00. The sails, anchors, and chains were sold for $196.74.

At least twenty of the granite blocks that the *Payton* carried can still be seen at low tide at the water's edge between Parking Lot #3 and Parking Lot #4 in Beavertail State Park. Others are submerged in nearby water.

Part IV

A Village and Its Inhabitants

Chapter 17

Water for the Village

As an island of farms with about four hundred people living on them, Conanicut Island had plenty of water. Natural springs fed ponds all over the island. Some farmers built dams on the streams to enlarge the ponds.

Even as the town developed as a resort, water was not a major concern. The first hotels used water from nearby streams, like the one that still flows in the gully between Brook and High Streets, and wells. Legend has it that Herbert F. Hammond kept fish in a stream that was fed from a spring under his hardware store. There was a town pump at the East Ferry from which village residents got water for daily use in their homes.

As the population grew and more houses were built in the small village area, more water was needed. The new steam-powered ferries needed fresh water as coolant. The amenities at the hotels, from indoor water closets to hydraulic elevators, needed water. Fire protection in the densely packed village became a concern. The purity of the available water—especially after the 1876 scare at Conanicut Park—was questioned.

The problem as Pardon Tucker, George C. Carr, and James H.M. Newlin saw it was not water availability but water distribution. The water was there, much of it accessible without digging wells. It just needed to be collected, stored, and distributed.

Pardon Tucker was a retired farmer who still lived on his farm just south of the village. He doesn't seem to have been interested in subdividing the farm, and for a while, it stood as open space between the village and summer cottages being built in the Dumplings. Tucker kept a close eye on the changes

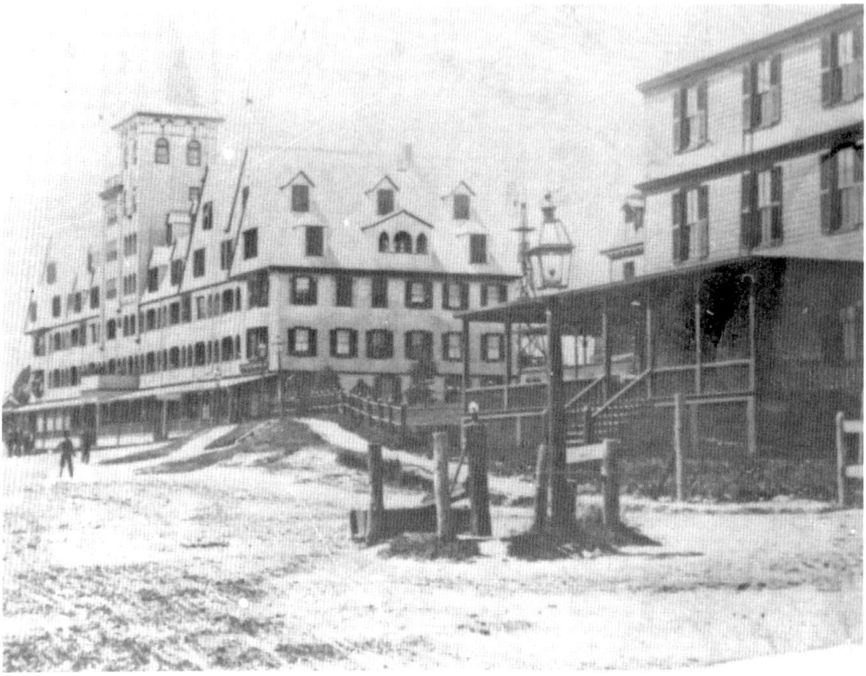

The town pump about 1892. The public pump stood in the middle of Conanicus Avenue at the end of Narragansett Avenue. *Jamestown Historical Society (P1973.005).*

around him. Recognizing both the need for pure water and, perhaps, the potential for profit without losing his open pastures, he helped found the Jamestown Light and Water Company in May 1888.

George C. Carr, the first president of the new corporation, was already deeply involved in the new developments in Jamestown. Fifteen years earlier, he had helped found the Jamestown & Newport Ferry Company, and he was president of the Ocean Highlands Land Company that developed the Dumplings area. He was for many years the president of the Jamestown Town Council.

The third member of the founding triumvirate was not a Jamestowner. He was a recently arrived summer visitor from Philadelphia. James H.M. Newlin seems to have been more interested in the "light" than the "water" in the company's name. A year before the company was founded, he, along with George C. Carr and two other summer Jamestowners, had requested that the town council erect lights on Narragansett and Walcott Avenues. He served on the town committee that addressed the lighting question, but he was never on the Jamestown Light and Water Company board. Actually,

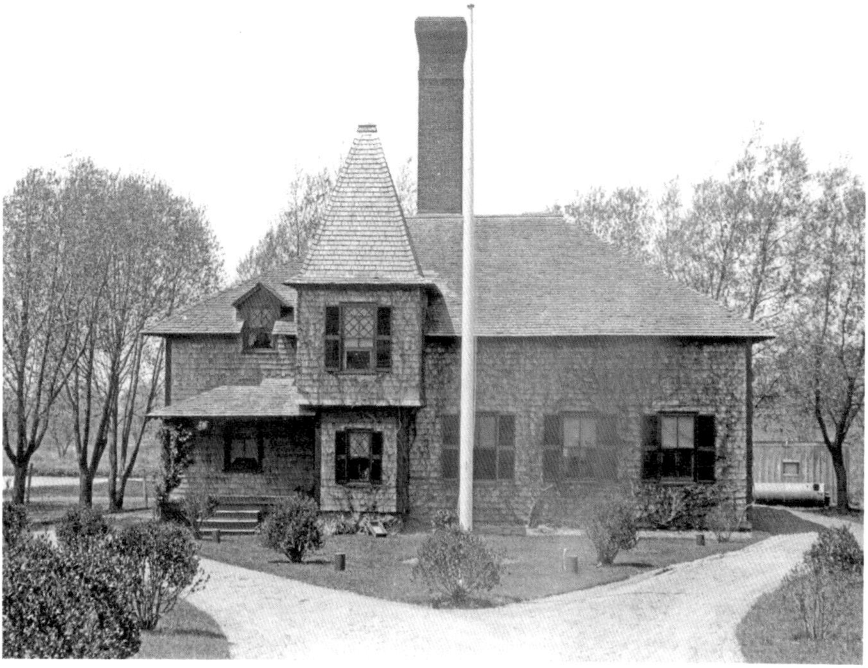

The Jamestown Water Company pumping station on Southwest Avenue at Clarke's Pond. *Jamestown Historical Society (P1965.080).*

the company never did have anything to do with lighting in the town, and eventually it became simply the Jamestown Water Company.

Planning began in earnest in late summer 1888. At first, the company contemplated a simple gravity feed from a reservoir on the higher ground at the south end of Green Lane to the hotels and houses along the waterfront. Within the year, hydrants to be used in case of fire and for flushing street sewers were added to the plan. The need for drinkable water in village homes, in the increasing number of hotels and guesthouses and in town hall—recently built on property higher than the intended reservoir—changed the basic requirements. A pumping station and a reservoir—larger than originally envisioned—were clearly necessary.

Spring 1890 saw the new plans coming together. The water would come from the pond at Clarke's icehouse on Southwest Avenue, "that being considered the purest and best." It would be raised by wind power to a standpipe located on top of the hill on Howland Avenue where the water towers are still. Gravity would force the water through pipes laid in the streets. The routes of the water mains would be negotiated with the town.

In mid-May 1890, at a special financial town meeting, it was decided—not without considerable controversy—that the town would purchase twenty hydrants. This action, as Thomas C. Clarke pointed out in his opposition statements, committed the town to supporting the new water system, although costs of building it remained with the privately owned Jamestown Water Company.

George Norman of Newport, a well-known builder of municipal waterworks in New England and beyond, presented a proposal to construct the complete waterworks. Water mains, not exceeding thirteen thousand feet, would provide water for all domestic and manufacturing uses at rates comparable to those charged by the Newport Water Works. Pipes would be laid in that part of town south of the crossroad leading to Cedar Cemetery from shore to shore. The main pipe was to run through Howland Avenue to High Street to Green Lane to Narragansett Avenue and then to Walcott along the shore, going north as far as Champlin's Hotel on Conanicus Avenue. Mains would go south to High Street and Walcott Avenue and extend as far west as the churches on Narragansett Avenue.

Norman would furnish and connect twenty-five hydrants and supply water to the town for sprinkling streets and flushing sewers at a cost not exceeding fifteen cents per one thousand gallons. The town was to pay the sum of thirty dollars per year for each hydrant. Option was also given to the town to purchase the waterworks in its entirety after twenty years.

The town's commitment to the plan was secured at a town meeting on June 2. Work began at once on the reservoir, the pumping station on Southwest Avenue, and the standpipe/water tower on Howland Avenue. By August 30, 1890, water was pumped into the standpipe, and the water was turned on for the takers.

The *Newport Journal* reported, "There will probably be no lack of water for consumers in Jamestown hereafter." The statement was proven false almost immediately. Water usage was so high that in 1899 sanctions were threatened. Before the end of the century, the Jamestown Water Company acquired two new ponds—now the South and North Reservoirs—to try to keep up with the increasing demand. In 1914, when the twenty-four-year-old metal standpipe on Howland Avenue began to leak, a new concrete tower was built. The new tower held 250,000 gallons, an increase of more than 20 percent over the original tank, and served the town for almost sixty years.

The Jamestown Water Company remained a privately run corporation until 1970 when the town purchased it for $300,000.

Chapter 18

The Reverend Preston and His Movable Chapel

Moving buildings from one place to another is a time-honored tradition in Jamestown—and it seems to have applied especially to places of worship. The Quakers moved their first meetinghouse from Eldred Avenue to Weeden Lane in 1734, although they had to replace that building in 1786 after the British effectively destroyed it. The Episcopalians purchased the multi-denominational church that stood in the Artillery Ground, near where the Jamestown Museum is now, and moved it across the street. They used it as a church hall after they built a new church in 1880.

The Central Baptists built their first chapel at the corner of Narragansett and Southwest Avenues in 1868. By 1890, they had outgrown the original building. It was moved to Cole Street to become the home of Mount Zion African Methodist Episcopal (AME) Church, and the present church was built on the lot. The AME church is now a private residence. The Catholics built their Chapel-by-the Sea on Clinton Avenue in 1892 and moved it to Narragansett Avenue in 1909 to become St. Mark Church.

One Jamestown religious structure was built to be moved regularly: the Episcopal Chapel of the Transfiguration, commonly known as the Movable Chapel.

For sixty years after its formation in 1836, St. Matthew's was part of Newport's Trinity Parish. In 1896, the congregation voted to become independent and self-supporting. The Reverend Charles E. Preston was appointed the first resident rector. Preston turned out to be an intriguing choice.

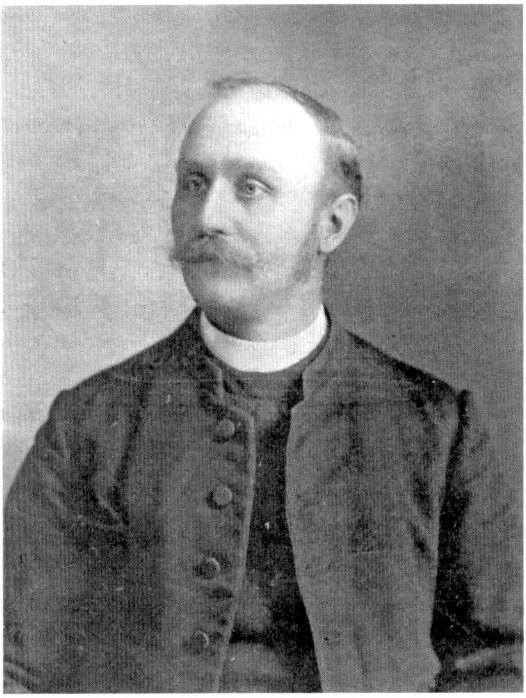

Left: Reverend Charles E. Preston, the driving force behind the building of the movable chapel. *Jamestown Historical Society (A2006.168.001).*

Below: Charles L. Bevins's design for the movable chapel. Bevins designed many of Jamestown's summer homes, especially in the Dumplings area. *Jamestown Historical Society (A2006.168.001).*

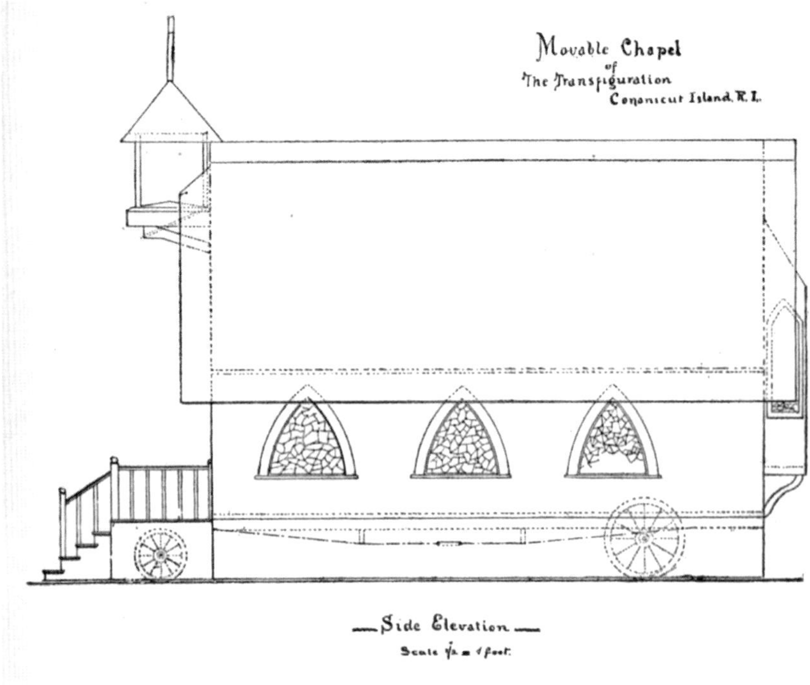

He was thirty-six years old when he arrived in Jamestown from St. Thomas's church in Providence with his second wife, Jennie—his first had died in childbirth—and two young sons, Earle and Carleton. Although according to later reports his record-keeping left much to be desired, he threw himself into both church and town activities.

In 1898, long before the advent of the house trailer or the RV, Preston conceived the idea of a church on wheels. Automobiles were still rare, and parishioners sometimes found getting to St. Matthew's difficult; the chapel would bring church services to them. For ten months of the year, it would sit about three miles north of the village and serve the year-round farm community. In the summer, it would be moved to the northernmost part of the island to serve the summer residents at Conanicut Park.

The chapel, designed by Jamestown architect Charles L. Bevins, was eighteen feet wide, and from the floor to the ridgepole, it stood eighteen feet high. The cross and belfry added several more feet. Inside, pews could seat one hundred people. George Barber began construction in 1898 in a lot next to St. Matthew's church. He brought in a railroad car to use as an office and storage area; the car was later moved to Beavertail, just north of the light, as a fishing camp and refreshment stand.

By Christmas, work on the movable chapel was practically finished. In April 1899, the completed chapel was moved, with great difficulty, by ten yoke of oxen recruited from Jamestown and Middletown to a spot on East Shore Road. The short trip took two days. There it remained—used as a chapel for at least part of the time—for ten years. In 1909, it was moved to North Main Road near Carr Lane. It never did reach Conanicut Park.

Charles Preston in the meantime became the center of a very public scandal. Soon after the completion of the chapel, he self-published, at great personal expense, *The First Movable Church: The Chapel of the Transfiguration, Conanicut Island*, a 136-page history of the building of the chapel with a large number of photographs. The cost of the book and of his personal investment in the chapel exceeded his financial assets.

On October 6, 1899, Preston took the ferry to Newport, boarded a train for Fall River, and got on the *Puritan*, a Fall River Line steamer bound for New York. He never arrived. The *New York Times* reported that officials found his gold watch and chain, wearing apparel, and letters addressed to prominent people in Jamestown and Newport in his cabin. One of the letters was not sealed and said that he was experiencing financial problems and asked that his family be notified. Suicide was assumed.

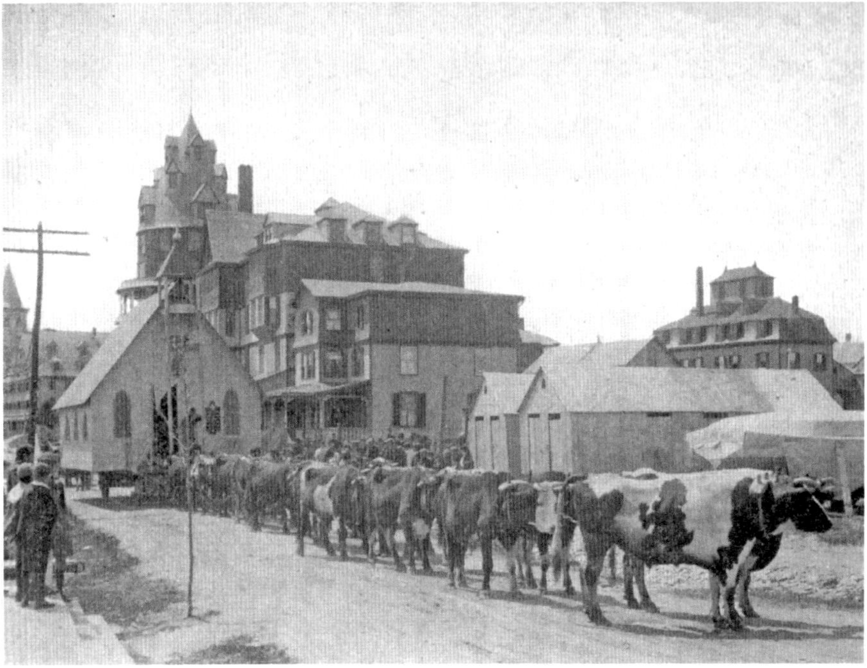

The movable chapel, drawn by ten yoke of oxen, on Conanicus Avenue in front of the Bay View Hotel in 1899. *Jamestown Historical Society (A2006.168.001).*

Preston, however, was not dead. A short time later, he was spotted in the company of Emma Moss, a schoolteacher half his age whom he had known in Providence and recruited for the Jamestown school. Preston's wife divorced him in a highly publicized and bitter court battle.

Emma and Charles Preston married in 1901. The couple moved often, tending westward, as Preston found temporary positions as a Methodist minister. Four children were born: John in 1901 in New Hampshire, Leah in 1903 in New York City, Ellis in 1905 in New Jersey, and Paul in 1908 in Illinois. They settled in 1917 in Edmonds, Washington, on the Pacific Coast just north of Seattle, and Preston died in Seattle in 1931 at the age of seventy-one. Emma outlived him by almost forty years, dying in 1970. She was ninety-three years old.

Georgina Day, a summer Jamestowner, purchased the unused chapel in 1933. Tom Preece, using a special tractor with caterpillar treads, moved the building to Harbor Street, where it was converted to a private residence. The house, with many of the architectural features of the chapel still discernible, is still there.

Chapter 19

Number, Please

Imagine life without the telephone. No way to call the fire department or police. If you wanted to chat with a friend on the other side of town, you actually had to go to the house. In 1850, with only fifty-four horses on the island and most of them at work in the fields, walking was often the only way to get there. You could go for days and see only the members of your family.

But that's the way the world was before Alexander Graham Bell invented the telephone in 1876.

Practical implementations of the new technology followed quickly. Within three years, Newport had a telephone exchange of its own with more than two hundred subscribers.

In the early 1880s, Jamestown boasted several large hotels, as well as boardinghouses, summer rental properties, and a growing number of private cottages owned by wealthy families. Local businessmen were on the lookout for ways to attract more summer visitors. They saw telephone service as just such an inducement.

In October 1882, developers from Jamestown and Newport circulated the prospectus for the Conanicut Telegraph and Telephone Company. They proposed a line from Conanicut Park to the Dumplings, and from there a cable to Fort Adams and a connection to the Newport exchange. The estimated cost was $3,500, but as a hedge against possible over-runs, $5,000 capital funding was sought with the sale of fifty $100 shares. By May 1883, a sufficient number of subscribers had pledged support to assure success of the project.

At a special town meeting, Jamestown residents voted the necessary authority to erect poles to carry the wires, and by July 16, the line from Conanicut Park to Fort Dumpling was complete. The modern equipment gave the island "a very businesslike appearance," according to the *Newport Daily News*. The cable between the Dumplings and Fort Adams was laid, and on August 18, the *Newport Journal* announced that a telegraph line between the Western Union office in Newport and offices in Jamestown and Conanicut Park was working, "and it is expected that the early introduction of the telephone will follow."

Unfortunately, it did not. Most of the blame fell on the cable under the bay, as the *Newport Daily News* reported in July 1885: "There has always been more or less trouble with the cable although the electric current seems to have been intact about three weeks ago. The cable is probably an imperfect one, or the trouble may be in the manner in which it was laid." Or perhaps where it was laid. While laying the cable at the narrowest point between the two islands may have seemed like a good idea, its position subjected the cable to the strongest tidal currents.

The next attempt to bring the telephone to Jamestown was made in 1893. At the March 15 town meeting, Walter A. Wright, the manager of the Newport Telephone Company and general agent for the Providence Telephone Company, presented a proposal by the Providence company to lay a "six wire, or double current, steel armored cable" from Coasters Island to the foot of Weeden Lane—clearly a more hospitable location than the Dumplings area—and requested permission to erect and maintain a telephone line from there to the Thorndike Hotel at East Ferry. The request was granted, "provided that the said Company erect suitable painted poles, thirty feet high." (These were the days before pressure-treated wood. The poles were painted green.) Originally there were to be two public telephones, one in the hotel for the convenience of the summer visitors and one for year-round use in John E. Watson's grocery store. But the company would extend the line to anyone who wished to subscribe, at a charge of about forty dollars a year for rental of the phone.

On May 16, 1894, at 5:15 p.m., Walter Wright called Charles E. Weeden, manager of the Thorndike Hotel, to check the circuit. It was good. The line was open for business. That was a Thursday, and as a bit of smart publicity, the company announced that there would be no charge for Jamestown calls until the following Monday. With such an inducement, many Jamestowners who had never before used a telephone enjoyed the novel experience of talking to friends in Newport, Providence, and even as far away as Pawtucket.

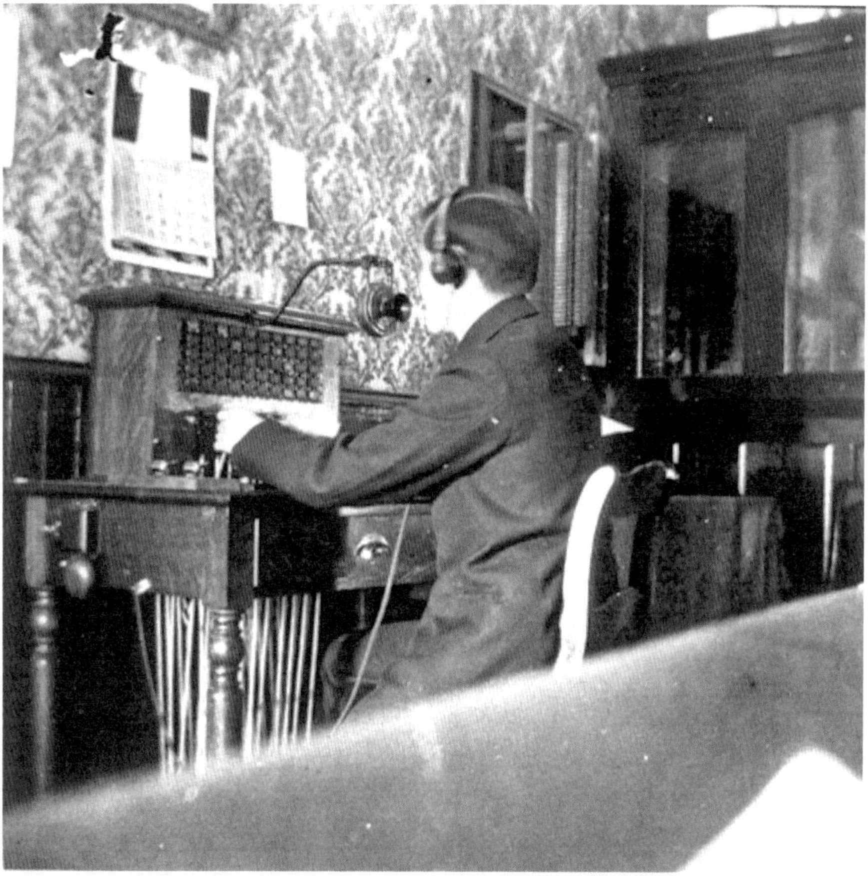

An operator at the summer switchboard in the Gardner House. Most of the night shift operators were young men. *Jamestown Historical Society (P1986.092).*

By 1901, the number of subscribers and the volume of business allowed a local switchboard to be set up in the writing room at the Gardner House. When the hotel closed for the winter, so did the switchboard, and the Newport exchange took over again.

This lack of local service in the winter soon became a source of annoyance and concern to Jamestown residents. If the Newport exchange was busy, it was hard to get calls through. Emergency calls to the police or fire department could be seriously delayed, as happened when a stable at Conanicut Park burned down. "Owing to there being no central office on the island in the winter and the necessity of the connection being made through the Newport central and that a score or more at various points on the island and different parts of Newport had seen the illumination and almost simultaneously had sought the telephone for information, more or less of a tangle resulted and it was some time before an alarm was turned in," reported the *Newport Journal*.

Prompted by continuing complaints, the town council, meeting in April 1913, penned a formal request to the Providence Telephone Company to establish a year-round Jamestown exchange and to include Newport in the local zone. At the time, it cost ten cents for a three-minute call to Newport. The company was not responsive, saying, "We have carefully considered the request made by your committee and find that the amount of business receipts does not warrant our keeping the exchange open the entire year." But as a concession, the charge for a call to Newport—which included calls to Jamestown through the Newport exchange—was reduced to five cents for five minutes.

This was appreciated, but it was not enough. Grumbling continued. In January 1914, Walter Wright, as representative of the Providence Telephone Company, was invited to a special public meeting convened by the town council to express the general dissatisfaction with the situation. Complaints were vigorously voiced: service was undependable, there was no year-round local exchange, instruments were old fashioned. Jesse Tefft, the fire chief, drew attention to the fact that he was on a three-party line—not a good set-up for emergency calls. Wright listened sympathetically and said he hoped soon "to comply with the wishes of the people of Jamestown."

Two months passed without any sign of a response to this outpouring of complaint. The town council decided to push and appointed Isaac Clarke, Adolphus Knowles, and Ralph Hull to follow up. Whether this committee stirred the telephone company to action or not, in June all the makings for an up-to-date telephone exchange arrived on the island. It was set up in an upstairs back room in the Gardner House. Jamestown had at last its own year-round exchange. Sarah Jane (Jennie) Clarke, Bessie Sheehan, and Lila Merritt were three of the earliest operators, and they continued to serve at this new switchboard.

Male operators took over on the night shifts. One of these was Fred C. Caswell, who held the position during his last years at Rogers High School and for a few years after graduation. A number of other night operators were also high school students.

The new Gardner House exchange served for eight more years. Then in 1922, the telephone company, no longer the Providence Telephone Company but the New England Telephone and Telegraph Company, bought Alton Coggeshall's hardware store. Coggeshall had built the small

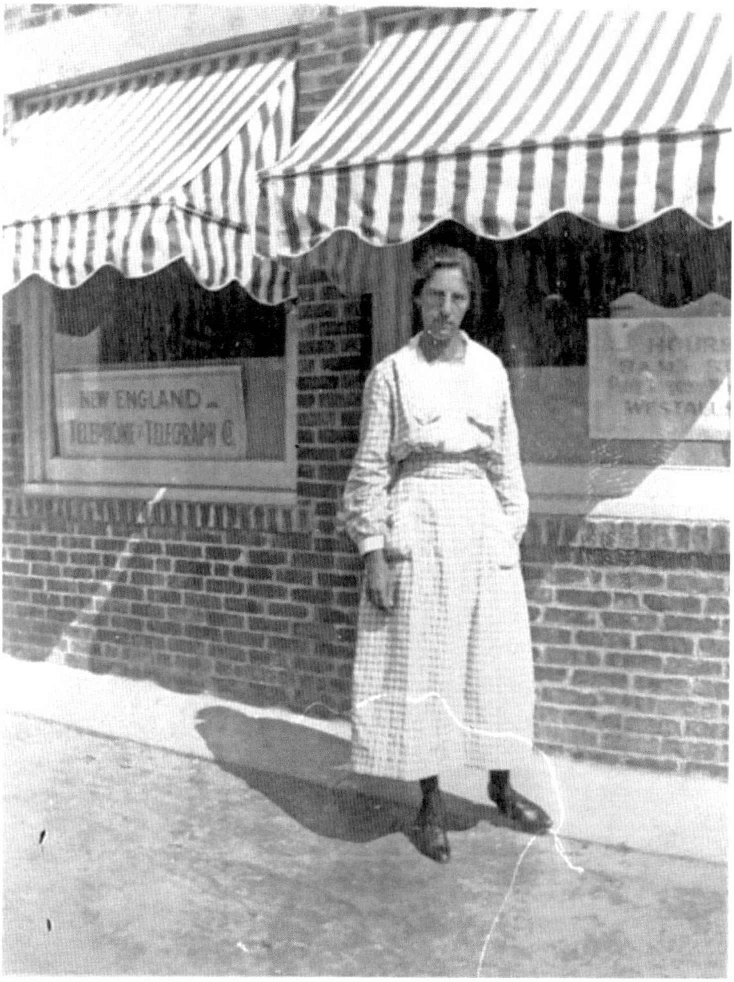

Sarah Jane (Jennie) Clarke, supervisor and then chief operator for the New England Telephone & Telegraph Co. in Jamestown. *Jamestown Historical Society (P1982J.016).*

brick building that still stands on the northeast corner of Narragansett Avenue and Coronado Street only about a year earlier. Presumably he was made an offer that he couldn't refuse.

The telephone company built an extension at the back to house equipment and batteries and for storage. In the front immediately to the left of the door was the supervisor's desk. Beyond that, running south to north along the east wall, was the five-position switchboard. Normally, two operators would be on duty, but at busy times in the summer, all the chairs might be occupied.

Young people who have only used dials or touch buttons to get their number may find it difficult to appreciate the role played by telephone operators in a small town. Hearing a voice say, "Number, please!" when you lifted the receiver made the telephone company a far more human institution. You got to know the operators, which ones might be short with you, which ones could be chatted up. And the operators certainly got to know a great deal about the callers—who their particular friends were, what some of their problems might be, and which ones might become irritable if their connection did not go through quickly. Though they were professionally discrete, they were both a repository and a source of town gossip and information. They would tell you where the fire was or what was going on at the church or whether so-and-so was back from the hospital. If the person you called in an emergency was not at home, they could often tell you where she or he might be. They would chat with you if you stopped by and they were not too busy. By all accounts, they enjoyed their job and enjoyed their engagement in the life of the town.

The end came in 1964 with the introduction of direct dialing. After fifty years of twenty-four-hour local and personal service, many found the change traumatic. As one former operator put it, "I never thought I'd lose my job to a robot."

Direct dialing is faster than going through an operator, and touch tone is even more efficient. Still, there are many Jamestowners who look back with unconcealed nostalgia to the slower, less efficient days of Jamestown's own highly personal telephone exchange.

Chapter 20

Necessity and Invention

According to the old English proverb, necessity is the mother of invention. When you want something badly enough, you will find a way to get it. Jamestowners have been inventing—and sometimes patenting—gadgets and methods for doing things since at least the middle of the nineteenth century.

The earliest patents referred to in Jamestown records were issued to Lucius Crandall for a crutch/shavings burner. He mentioned the patents in his will, so to him at least they were important parts of his estate. Exactly what the patents entailed is unknown.

William G. Knowles was one of the early captains for the Jamestown & Newport Ferry Company, guiding the new steam ferries back and forth across the East Passage until his death in 1883. How and why he got interested in clothes washing is a mystery—perhaps his wife, the former Mary Slocum, complained about raw hands caused by rubbing the heavy clothes he wore at sea against a washboard. Whatever the impetus, in 1872, he was issued a patent for a new washing machine designed to keep the clothes washer's hands out of the water and, perhaps, make the task less strenuous.

In his patent application, he explained the new machine in words and pictures.

> *This invention relates to a new washing machine in which a reciprocating slotted washboard is arranged to move on spring-rails under and against friction-rollers that hang in a spring-frame…The articles to be cleaned are…interposed between the washboard and said rollers, and the crankshaft next turned with suitable rapidity. This will cause the board to rub against*

the rollers and to act on the goods in a manner necessary to effect the desired cleaning process.

The machine sounds like an adaptation of the wringers that were used to press water from the clothes as you removed them from the water. The energy to get the clothes clean was still provided by human beings, but at least they could keep their hands dry while they did it.

Daniel "Real Estate Dan" Watson, one of Jamestown's first real estate agents, managed to combine an interest in mechanical things with his real estate business. In 1887, he patented a door fastener to be used when there was no lock or when the lock was broken or the key lost. The invention was certain to be of use to real estate agents, especially in a resort community such as Jamestown at the end of the nineteenth century.

Like Knowles, Henry Armbrust was one of the large number of Jamestowners associated with the Jamestown & Newport Ferry Company. His grandfather Peter, a ferry captain who later commanded an army ship servicing the local forts, had settled in Jamestown in 1877, and Henry grew up on the island. He studied chemistry and biology in college and worked for many years for the Builder's Iron Foundry in New Hampshire. When he left the company in 1967, he opened his own water consulting business, providing expert advice on water usage in swimming pools, municipal water systems, porpoise pools, and pools in major zoos and marine projects.

Along with two other chemists, Henry Armbrust developed a new water purification process for small water systems. The new process, which used a two-pump system for chlorine dioxide treatment, required a long-term test. The test was conducted at the Jamestown Water Company, and the system was so successful that the town continued to use it for many years after.

Armbrust also held a patent for a method for cleaning a submerged surface, such as the walls of a swimming pool or aquarium, without draining the pool:

I provide a wall which may have flanges extending therefrom to engage and seal against the surface to be cleaned and enclose an area to be treated, and I provide connections through this wall by which the water entrapped by the flanged wall may be withdrawn and the area to be cleaned flushed with a chemical for cleaning the surface by filling the evacuated space so as to treat or clean the segregated surface area without the chemical contaminating the water of the pool.

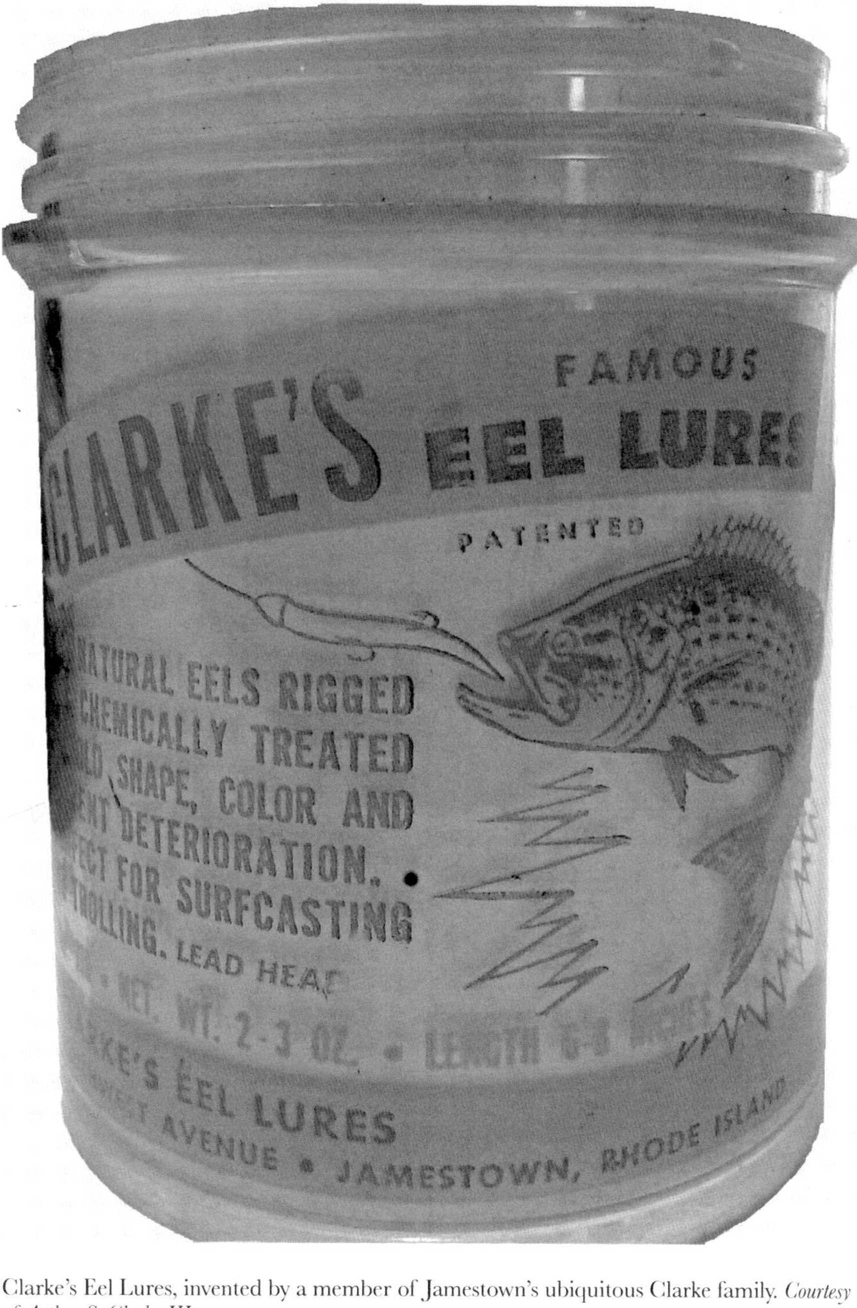

Clarke's Eel Lures, invented by a member of Jamestown's ubiquitous Clarke family. *Courtesy of Arthur S. Clarke III.*

Once the segregated area was cleaned, the flanged wall could be moved to a different area and the process repeated.

Water—this time saltwater—also figured in an invention by Arthur S. Clarke. He was a descendant of Joseph Clarke, whose name appears in the original pre-purchase agreement for Conanicut and Dutch Islands.

Clarke owned Clarke's Marina and Ship Appliances and was an ardent sportsman and fisherman. He is credited with landing the largest striped bass ever caught off Jamestown in 1936. His contribution to the art of fishing was the Clarke's Eel Lure. The lures, put together in a garage at the family's business site on Southwest Avenue, contained real eels, chemically treated to prevent deterioration and to retain the original color. The lures were particularly adapted to surfcasting for striped bass from the many rocks along the Jamestown shore.

From fishing to sailing is not much of a jump for Jamestowners, and sailing—or rather the filming of sailing boats—was the inspiration for the invention of the Biddlestick. John Scott Biddle, a member of a Philadelphia family that had summered in Jamestown since the 1880s, was a videographer who during the second half of the twentieth century filmed "everything from wind surfers to tall ships." One problem he often faced was holding his camera steady, especially when both he and his subject were moving erratically with the wind.

To provide more stability, he invented the Biddlestick. The device is a fifteen-inch-long, one-inch-thick aluminum tube that can be screwed into the bottom of a camcorder or a still camera. Bracing the Biddlestick against the operator's forearm or chest steadies the camera. The device also makes it possible to hold and operate the camera with one hand while using the other to hold on and keep one's balance in a maneuvering sailboat.

Another use for the Biddlestick has evolved. A recent eBay offering of the Biddlestick called it a "short selfie stick."

Very few twenty-first-century inventions are patented in a single name, but Jamestowners are listed prominently on a number of recent patent applications. Bruce E. Wigton, Emma Amelia Durand, and Richard B. Dunne, all from Jamestown, are named as principals in a series of patents for a counterflow insect trap. The device they designed attracts and captures flying insects such as mosquitoes, no-see-ums, and other insects that are attracted to components of sweat and breath emanating from mammals. Placed in a corner of a yard away from where people congregate, the insect trap can attract the unwanted flying insects to that area and entice them into a confined space where they can be easily destroyed—a definite plus for outdoor entertaining in Jamestown during the summer.

Jamestowner Aidan Petrie makes his living inventing. He's the chief innovation officer at Ximedica, a design firm he helped found in 1985. The firm specializes in designing medical products, and in a September 2014 *Rhode Island Monthly* interview, Petrie emphasized that his designs all incorporate the concept that form follows function. "If granny has to use something and her eyesight is going, then you have to design the product in a way that's appropriate for her needs," he explained.

Among Petrie's most recent innovations are a decorative pill splitter, a rectal thermal monitor, and a portable pneumatic controller and battery configuration that makes connection between the two components easier for busy clinicians in an emergency situation.

Martin Keen, the founder of Focal Upright Furniture, absolutely agrees with Petrie's emphasis on form following function, although his interests have taken him in an entirely different direction. Keen worked for many years as a shoe designer. In 2003, he patented the hybrid sandals that he had designed to protect his feet when he went sailboat racing and launched KEEN® Footwear.

Most of his design time was spent sitting uncomfortably on a stool or standing at his drafting table. He began to look for a more comfortable way to work. In 2012 and 2013, after—according to his company's website—twelve years, 456 drawings, forty-two scale models, and twenty working prototypes, he patented a desk and chair design that allows a person to work in a half sitting/half standing position. His ergonomically designed Locus Workstation won the December 2012 ErgoExpo award for best new product.

Chapter 21

Seeing the Light

Jamestown of the late nineteenth century was a town with two personalities. In the summer months, the resort hotels and seasonal cottages brought about 2,500 vacationers to the town. At the end of the season, these summer people packed off to Philadelphia, St. Louis, New York, and other cities around the country, leaving the one thousand full-time residents in a ghost town of shuttered buildings.

The summer folk brought with them ideas and demands that went beyond what the old-time farmers, who at the turn of the century still made up more than a quarter of the voters, thought necessary. Nowhere was this more evident than in the installation of streetlights.

Street lighting was a relatively new idea. Providence had first tried it in 1820 and experimented with at least four different fuels—whale oil, kerosene, gas, and gasoline—before installing the new electric lights early in the twentieth century. Rural communities saw no reason to follow the urban example. The farmer's day was governed by the sun. In addition, maintaining early streetlamps was expensive. Someone had to light each lamp individually in the evening and extinguish it in the morning.

Jamestown's summer residents, whose recreational activities were definitely not governed by the sun, wanted streetlights. In mid-July 1887, the town council received a formal petition from Robert B. King of St. Louis, Edward Roth and James H.M. Newlin of Philadelphia, and George C. Carr of Jamestown. The petition asked the town to install street lighting the length of Narragansett Avenue from East Ferry to West Ferry and on Walcott Avenue down to the

Dumplings. It suggested that the expense be defrayed by levying a special tax on the owners of property along the lighted streets.

The council appointed the petitioners to a committee to look into the matter. They reported back quickly and included an opinion from Francis Peckham, city solicitor of Newport, that the council had the authority to order the lighting and levy the suggested tax.

There the matter stood until the following summer. On August 1, 1888, a special meeting of the town council was held to listen to and act on the recommendations of a committee for public improvements. Three members of the committee were summer residents: Admiral David Dixon Porter, James H.M. Newlin, and James Hopkins. Two were year-round residents, both interested in the development of the town: George C. Carr and Pardon Tucker.

Newlin presented the case for lighting the streets. Two of his recommendations show a sensitivity to the aversion of the year-round residents to kowtowing to the summer community and to spending money unnecessarily. The expense of the lights would be covered by increased valuation of the property directly benefitting from the lights and not by an increase in taxes on the whole town, and the lamps would be lit "for at least four months in the year," i.e., during the summer months.

Admiral Porter spoke in favor of the recommendation and of the importance of streetlights. He also suggested that possibly the reason the people of Jamestown were not troubled with tramps was because it was so dark that even those undesirables were afraid.

The town council agreed to place naphtha lights—i.e., lamps that burned some form of liquid hydrocarbon—three hundred feet apart along the selected route. Within the week, workmen were putting in the posts, some fifty in all. The Globe Lighting Company of Boston had the contract to supply, light, and take care of the lamps at an expense to the town of ten cents a light per night.

All did not go quite smoothly, of course. For a few weeks, a game of place the lights/move the lights went on. The lamp opposite the pump at the East Ferry was moved to higher ground. The one at Green Lane was placed on the opposite corner. However, by August 11, Walcott Avenue, Brook and Union Streets, Narragansett Avenue, and part of the waterfront were lighted for the very first time. The *Newport Daily News* congratulated Newlin on the prompt and efficient fulfillment of his "pet scheme."

As agreed, the streetlamps were put away for the winter and placed back in position on their posts in mid-June 1889. And so it went for several years, with a few additional lights added almost every summer.

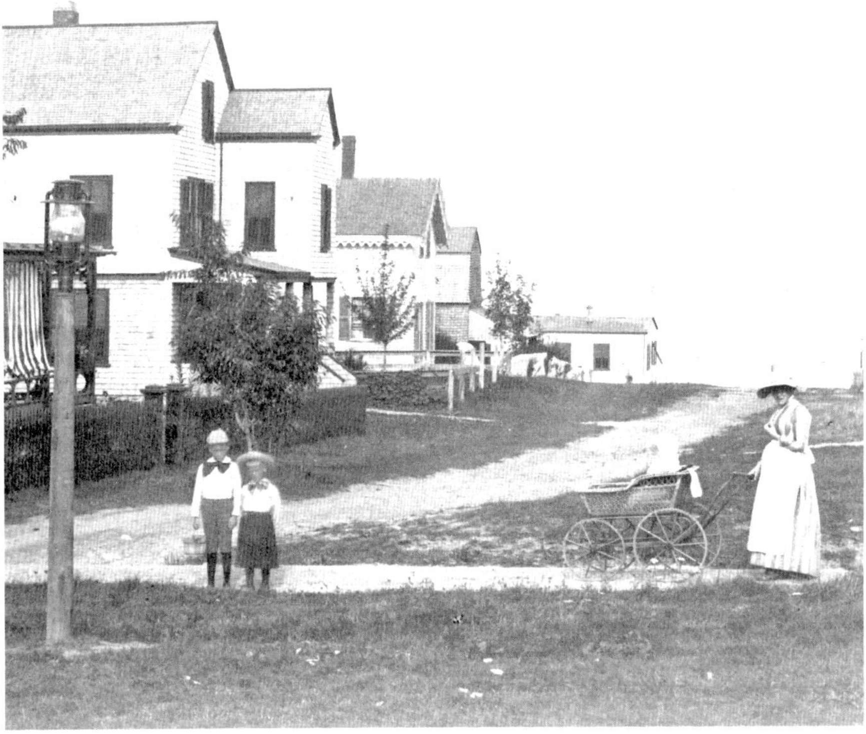

An early naphtha streetlight at Green Lane and Lincoln Street. *Jamestown Historical Society (P1981R.023).*

Not all Jamestowners were happy with the winter darkness. In October 1890, forty residents and taxpayers petitioned the town council asking that the streetlights be left in place year round. In November 1896, the *Newport Journal* reported that some young women of the town were willing to light and take care of the street lamps provided the town furnished the oil.

Some of the town's reluctance to expand the system of oil lamps was understandable. Electric lights were obviously the direction to go, and since 1890, proposals to electrify the town had been floating around.

After almost ten years of inaction by the town, the hotels moved independently toward electrification. In 1899, Patrick H. Horgan, owner of the Thorndike Hotel, contracted with the Fairbanks Company of Boston for a twenty-five-horsepower gasoline engine to furnish power for some two hundred lights in his hotel, three cottages, and the hotel stores. Owners of the Gardner House joined in, buying a twenty-seven-horsepower engine for lighting and to operate their elevator. The Knowles family at the Bay View followed suit. Electric lights were in place at the first two hotels by early July.

Ten years later, the town was still wrestling with the problem. Electricity was still not available publicly, although individuals as well as the hotels had their own small power plants. In April 1910, Dr. W. Lincoln Bates, president of the Dr. Bates Sanitarium Company, presented a petition asking for an extension of the existing oil lamp system. He wanted lights to be maintained year-round on Conanicus Avenue from the Bay View Hotel as far up as the Gardiner Cottage, just north of the sanitarium across from the Bay Voyage Hotel. The next month, the town council approved payment for year-round lights in the compact part of town. Lighting in Conanicut Park continued to be seasonal.

Electricity was still the acknowledged long-term solution. Early in 1912, the Newport Illuminating Company proposed to supply power to the island from its Newport plant through a cable across the lower end of the bay. "The Bay State Company [the parent company to Newport Illuminating Company] agrees to maintain two cables or one cable and an auxiliary plant within the town, so that in case of accident the town will not be without lights for any length of time," reported the *Electric Spark*, the newssheet put out by Dr. Bates Sanitarium.

Despite some legal conflicts, an agreement giving the Newport Illuminating Company an exclusive franchise to supply electric current for light, heat, and power was approved at a special town council meeting on December 14, 1912, and confirmed at the financial town meeting in June 1913.

Construction of the distribution system had begun before the June financial town meeting. The village had electric streetlights by July.

Chapter 22

Nurserymen and Florists

In the late nineteenth and early twentieth centuries, agriculture became less and less important in Jamestown's economy as summer hotels and vacation homes were built on land that had once been farmland and pasture. One form of agriculture flourished, perhaps because it catered to the newcomers. Nurserymen and florists established hothouses and gardens, providing flowers, shrubs, and seedlings to customers from Boston to New York. None of these new agriculturists came from established Jamestown families. All were transplants—mostly immigrants from northern Europe.

The first to arrive was Samuel Smith. He was born in England and immigrated to Georgia in 1853. He acquired a plantation on the St. Johns River in Florida and seems to have been doing well there when the American Civil War began in April 1861. He came north to avoid the war and settled in Newport.

He and a partner, Michael Butler, erected greenhouses on Bellevue Avenue and began a florist business that catered to the social elite who summered in Rhode Island. The firm also opened a branch in New York, one of only five florist shops in the city at the time. According to family lore, Smith introduced the gardenia to the florist industry, which considering his ten years in the South is definitely possible.

Smith moved his florist business to Jamestown in the 1870s. He built greenhouses behind his house on Narragansett Avenue from which he supplied florist shops in Boston, Providence, and Newport. The 3,200 square feet of glass enclosing his greenhouses rated a special note in the state report on agriculture in Jamestown in 1885.

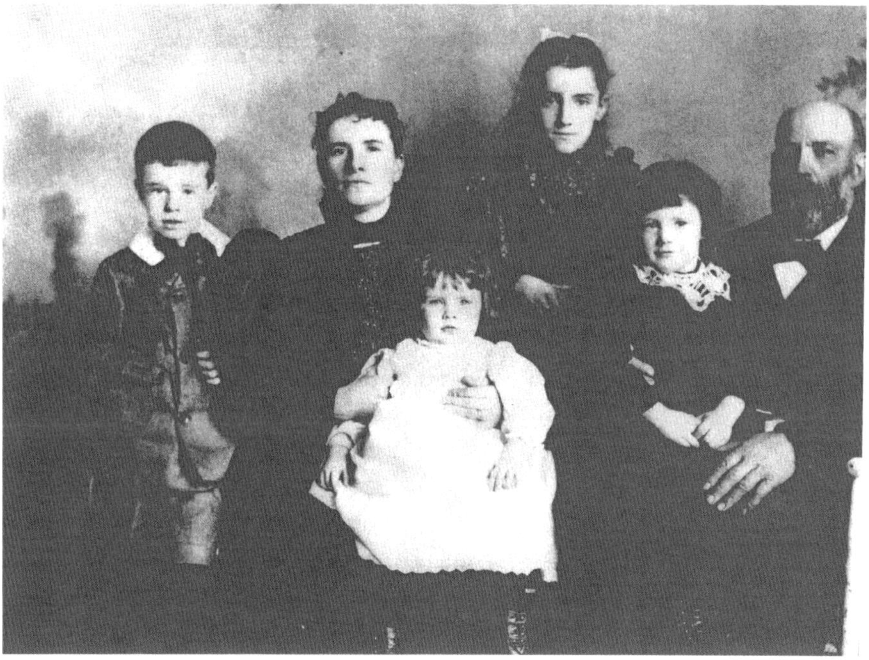

Samuel Smith family in 1895. *Left to right*: Samuel Smith Jr. (1889–1962), Bridget (Delia) Murphy Smith (1864–1933) holding Mary Alice (1894–1967), Anna (1885–1964), Jayne (1891–1967) on lap of Samuel W. Smith (1834–1932). *Jamestown Historical Society (P2009.030.004).*

In 1890, Samuel brought his eighteen-year-old nephew Albert Boone over from England to help with his growing business. Six years later, the young man married Anna Mary Skelley (sometimes spelled Skelly), an Irish woman eight years his senior, and at the turn of the century, the family lived in the Greene farmhouse on Longfellow Road on Shoreby Hill. (The Greene farmhouse is one of the few Colonial houses that survived the British occupation during the American Revolution.) Boone was primarily known as a landscape gardener, and from 1930 to 1946, he managed a number of Shoreby Hill estates.

Smith continued in the florist business until about ten years before his death in 1932 at the age of ninety-seven. His sons Samuel Jr. (1889–1962) and John (1897–1988) took over and expanded the business.

The Smiths built greenhouses at the end of Clinton Avenue at least as early as 1921. In the spring of 1928, the firm—now Samuel Smith Sons—built a new 209- by 45-foot greenhouse near the other greenhouses on Clinton Avenue. In 1929, it added a central heating plant designed to supply all the greenhouses

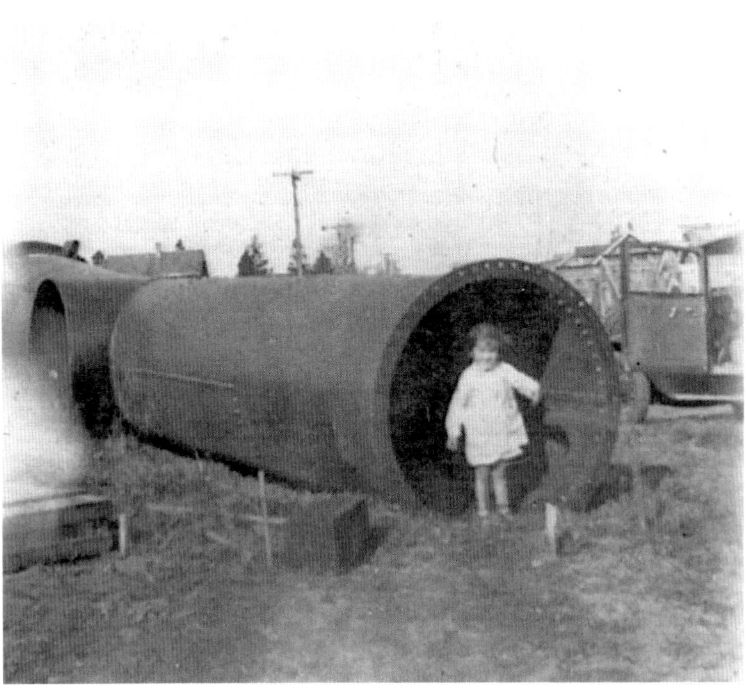

John L. Smith's daughter, Katherine Smith Murphy, in front of a smokestack during greenhouse construction. *Jamestown Historical Society (P2004M.354).*

with heat. The large steel smokestack for the plant weighed ten tons and towered 90 feet high. Two more 60- by 110-foot steel-framed greenhouses were added to the complex early in May 1930. The greenhouses were almost completely destroyed during the Hurricane of 1938.

Scottish-born David Gordon was twenty-six when he arrived in New York on September 12, 1885. Like Smith, he came to Jamestown by way of Newport, where he worked as a gardener for the Lorillards on Ochre Point before Pierre Lorillard IV sold the property to Cornelius Vanderbilt in 1892 and the current Breakers was built. Gordon and his wife, Mary, moved to Jamestown in 1891. Behind his house that still stands at 99 Southwest Avenue, on a right of way that exists (unnamed) between Southwest Avenue and Pleasant View, he built a greenhouse. His wife died in 1899, leaving him with three sons—Adam, Louis, and William—all under the age of ten. His sister-in-law Emily Freeland came to live with the family, and for the next five years, Gordon worked in Jamestown as a florist and gardener, supplementing his income by selling books and stationery.

Gordon seems not to have been as successful as some of Jamestown's other early florists. About 1905, Gordon sold his house and greenhouse to Frank Jencek and moved to Westchester, New York.

Jencek (there are many variant spellings of his name: Jenceck, Jeneik, Jencik, Jancek) was born on April 20, 1866, in central Europe. Different records show his birthplace as Bohemia (1903), Austria (1910, 1915), Germany (1920), and Czechoslovakia (1930)—all of which may be accurate considering the changing map of Europe in the early twentieth century. Frank and his wife, Annette, arrived in New York in 1894 and moved to Jamestown in 1903. After buying David Gordon's house and greenhouses, they added to and practically rebuilt the greenhouses. Jencek engaged in market gardening and made early vegetables a specialty, although he also continued Gordon's florist business.

Blucher Tweed was the only one of Jamestown's early twentieth-century nurserymen to be born in the United States. Born in North Carolina, he wandered to Texas as a young man, and during World War I, he served as

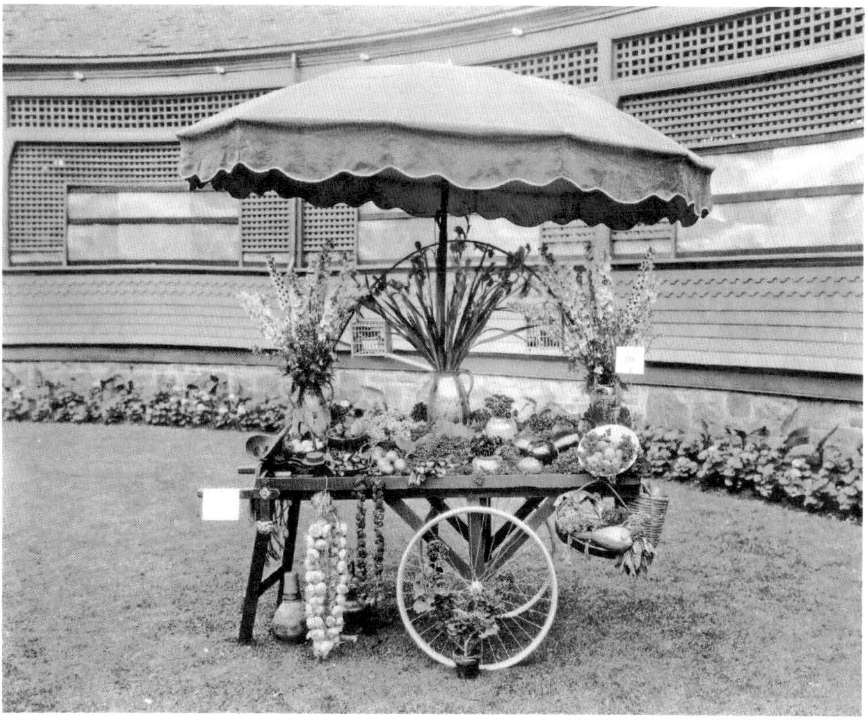

Jamestown Garden Club's first-place display at the Newport Garden Association Flower Show in July 1932. Frank Jencek and John L. Smith contributed flowers. *Jamestown Historical Society (O2010.021.004).*

an electrician first class in the navy. Soon after leaving the navy in 1921, he married Jenett (some records say Jeanette) Shelman, a Swedish immigrant, from Newport. Jenett's elder sister Martha was married to Arthur L. Hull of Jamestown, which is perhaps what drew the newlyweds to the island.

In 1922, the Tweeds bought a large plot of land that went from North Road to East Shore Road along the south side of Eldred Avenue and started a nursery. Unlike the Smiths, the Tweeds focused on plants that could be grown without extensive greenhouses. They grew evergreens and, in 1936, donated the community Christmas tree. They grew azaleas and similar garden bushes both for the flowers and to sell for planting.

Jenett Tweed was the town tree warden for most of the 1940s and into the early 1950s. As warden, she directed town efforts to control the Japanese beetle and to save the elm trees.

The Tweeds were also very interested in maintaining the character of Jamestown. When the extensive build-out in the Jamestown Shores area led the town to contemplate zoning changes in the early 1950s, they spoke in favor of more restrictive zoning. Jenett Tweed suggested that the building line be set back twenty-five feet from the road and indicated she would not transfer any of her property unless the buyer agreed to build Cape Cod–style structures in keeping with the locale.

John T. Scheepers does not properly belong in a list of Jamestown nurserymen since he did not have a nursery in Jamestown. He was, however, for several years a summer resident of Jamestown, and he was widely known as the "Tulip King."

Scheepers was a native of the Netherlands. He was sent to New York in 1901 to promote the Dutch tulip industry in America. In 1910, he married Rose Heywood of Boston, whose sister Alice was married to Benjamin S. Cottrell, who owned Fox Hill Farm. The Scheepers built a home on Fort Getty Road, and both families summered on the farm.

Scheepers was very successful in his mission to popularize the tulip in the United States. He also pioneered and was the first to display narcissi and to import tuberous-rooted begonias and amaryllis. He was so successful in establishing the Dutch bulb business in America that, in 1932, he was made a knight of the Order of Orange-Nassau by Queen Wilhelmina of Holland.

The company he founded, John Scheepers, Inc., to import and distribute flower bulbs is still in existence as Van Engelen Wholesale Flowers, which is run by his nephew and niece. The yellow tulips that bloom in the Artillery Lot next to the museum each spring are a variety that Scheepers developed called "Mrs. John T. Scheepers."

Part V

Our Military Neighbors

Chapter 23

Early Forts and Batteries

By itself, Jamestown has little military value. The Beavertail watchtower, the town's first pseudo-military installation, was built in 1705 primarily as a navigational aid for ships bound for Newport. It was also an observation post to give merchants in Newport early warning of intrusion, whether by a foreign power or a buccaneer.

The Eighteenth Century

The Conanicut Battery earthwork fortifications on the west side of Prospect Hill, built by order of the Rhode Island General Assembly in the spring of 1776, were designed to protect Newport from warships that might sail up the West Passage and attack the city from the north. By December 1776, when a British fleet of seventy ships *did* sail up the West Passage, Conanicut's cannon had already been withdrawn to Aquidneck Island, and no shots were fired. After securing Newport, the British quickly occupied the battery and held it for almost three years.

The only cannon the Jamestown colonists successfully fired during the American Revolution wasn't fired by the army but by a farmer, John Eldred. According to legend, Eldred, who owned a farm on the East Passage north of Potter's Cove, balanced a cannon barrel between two large boulders overlooking the entrance to Newport Harbor. Because he had some powder but no shot, he gathered appropriately sized rocks to use as cannon balls. He lobbed the rocks toward the British revenue ships as they went up and down the bay.

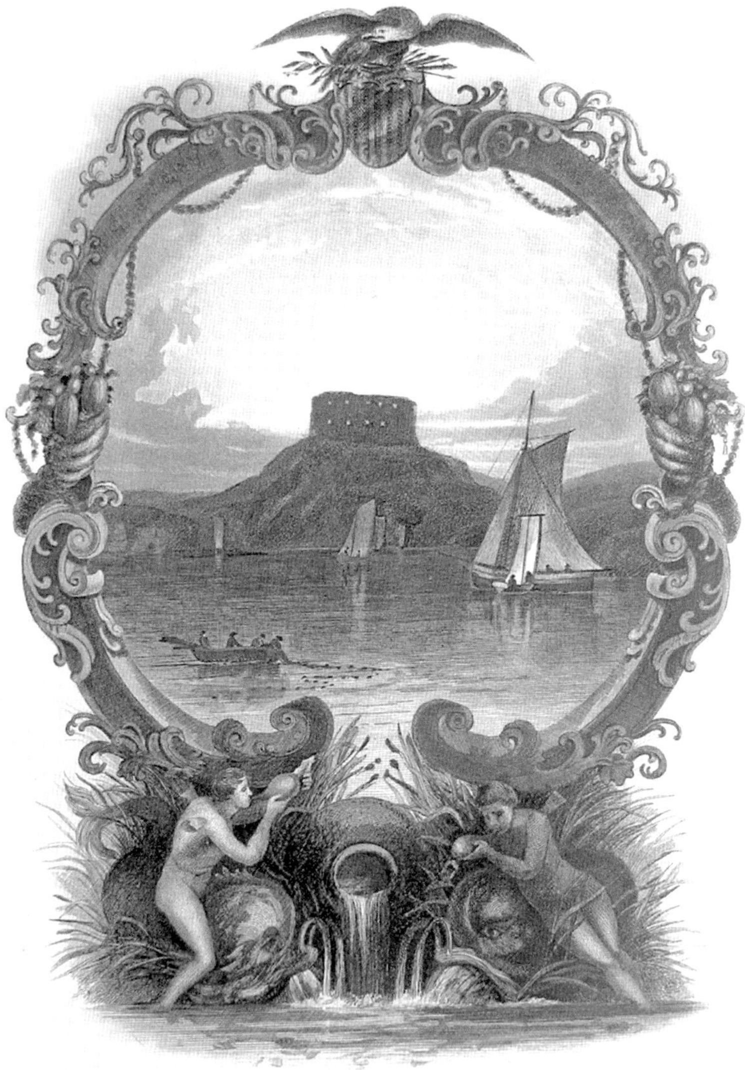

An engraving of Fort Dumpling based on an 1831 oil painting by William G. Wall and published by Samuel Walker, Boston. *Jamestown Historical Society (P1980.380).*

Most of the shots landed harmlessly in the water, but one tore out a mainsail. In response, the English sent a contingent ashore to make the cannon inoperable. Eldred avoided the landing party by fleeing to the safety of the marsh around the Great Creek.

After the Revolution, the island resumed its peaceful, if now less affluent, agricultural way of life, until once more privateering made the island's position at the entrance of Narragansett Bay convenient for the defense of the cities farther inland. In 1799, alarmed by French privateer raids on American shipping, the federal government purchased six and a half acres of land just south of Bull Point near the current site of the Fort Wetherill Boat Basin. Major Louis de Tousard of the Army Corps of Engineers, who also designed Fort Adams in Newport, directed the construction of a fort on the site. The structure was 108 feet long and 81 feet wide, and its walls varied in height between 12 and 24 feet, depending on the contours of the rock beneath. Originally called Fort Louis and later officially renamed Fort Brown, the oval stone fort was universally known as Fort Dumpling.

Fort Dumpling was never armed or maintained. In the mid- and late nineteenth century, the decaying stone pile was a popular tourist attraction and picnicking spot. It was not, however, safe. Soldiers at Fort Adams targeted the Fort Dumpling tower for both artillery and rifle practice, and on July 4, 1877, a rifleman at Fort Adams wounded a woman picnicking there. After that, both target practice and picnicking were forbidden, but that didn't stop the sightseers.

Almost one hundred years after it was built, the old tower was blown up to make way for construction of Fort Wetherill. According to an 1898 newspaper account, the explosion "threw a light cloud of dust and small stones into the air, and then apparently the side of the cliff tumbled into the water. About 70 feet of the face of the old fort went over with the rock immediately below it."

THE CIVIL WAR

Jamestown, too far from the action to be fortified during the War Between the States, was the site of two training camps.

The sixteen-acre Camp Meade sat south of Narragansett Avenue between Green Lane and Howland Avenue. About one thousand Third Rhode Island Cavalry recruits—none of them from Jamestown—trained at the camp between July 1, 1863, and November 25, 1865. The men in Camp Meade far outnumbered the residents of the village that surrounded it. They lived in their own separate world—and weren't very considerate of their hosts. At different times, the town complained that the horses stabled at the camp were "going at large on the public highways of Jamestown" and that the soldiers were "taking indiscriminately poultry and sheep and throwing down fences." The main body of the Third left Jamestown in late December 1863, although new recruits continued to be trained at the camp.

In 1863, 1,800 black soldiers from across New England were recruited for three-year enlistments. Camp Bailey on Dutch Island was built by the Fourteenth Rhode Island Heavy Artillery (Colored), Rhode Island's black regiment. The first units of the Fourteenth arrived on Dutch Island in early September 1863. They quickly constructed an eight-gun earthworks south of the center of the island. The Lower Battery, about seven hundred feet north of the Dutch Island light, was built next but was never armed because the site flooded.

An outbreak of smallpox during the winter of 1863–64 took the lives of fifteen of the men building the Dutch Island fortification. One man died of tetanus or gangrene after hitting his thumb with a hammer setting up his tent. The bodies were buried in a small cemetery on the northeast shore of the island. The remains were reburied on Long Island in 1948. The Fourteenth Rhode Island left the island early in 1864, serving primarily in Texas and Louisiana.

Until 1897, Dutch Island was practically deserted. In September 1889, only Ordinance Sergeant B.F. Morrell, as sole representative of the U.S. Army, guarded the remains of the Camp Bailey batteries.

ENDICOTT FORTIFICATIONS

In 1886, a report by William Endicott, President Grover Cleveland's Secretary of War, spelled out in detail the country's vulnerability to attack from the sea. It took almost a decade for plans to be made and for large-scale construction to begin. But between 1897 and 1906, three forts were built on Conanicut and Dutch Islands as part of a major effort to strengthen the country's coastal defences. Fort Greble on Dutch Island, Fort Getty on the West Passage, and Fort Wetherill on the East Passage were all constructed at this period.

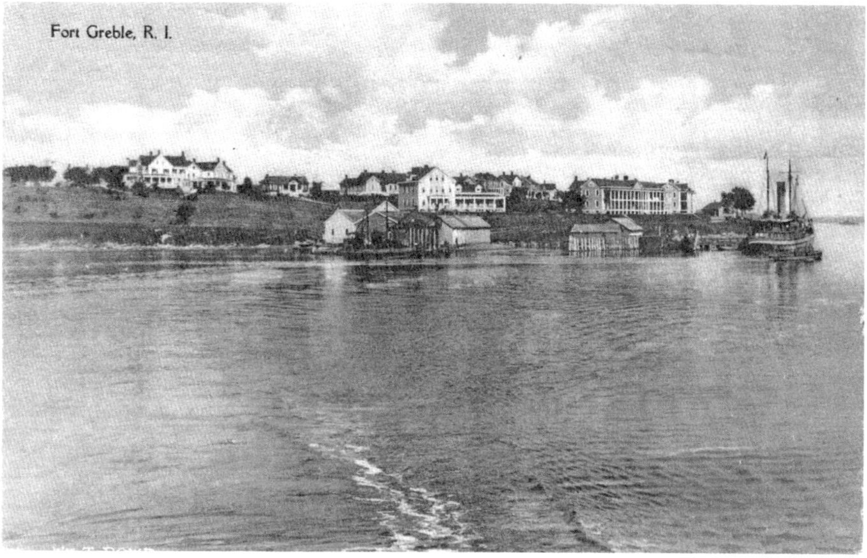

Postcard of Fort Greble showing the barracks (right), hospital (center), and administration and support buildings (on hill behind). *Jamestown Historical Society (P2015.113.014).*

The Dutch Island fortification began first—perhaps because the government already owned the land. Between 1897 and 1903, four batteries were constructed and equipped with weapons ranging from three-inch, fifteen-pound, rapid-fire guns to twelve-inch mortars.

From the beginning of the century through the mid-1920s, Dutch Island was home to a largely self-sufficient military community. Fort Greble had a post office, post exchange, bowling alley, bakery, tennis court, hospital, and accommodations for about five hundred personnel in addition to the permanent Coast Artillery cadre. The West Passage ferries stopped at the island, and the men stationed there also participated in the social activities in Jamestown village.

Unfortunately, vital supplies needed to be replenished from across the bay. In particular, there was inadequate on-site water. Water piped in from Saunderstown was stored in underground cisterns, and some of the West Passage ferryboats were designed with special water tanks to bring water to the fort.

The advances in air warfare during and after World War I made the batteries at Fort Greble obsolete. They had no anti-air capability, and they were not built to be camouflaged against air attack. The disadvantages

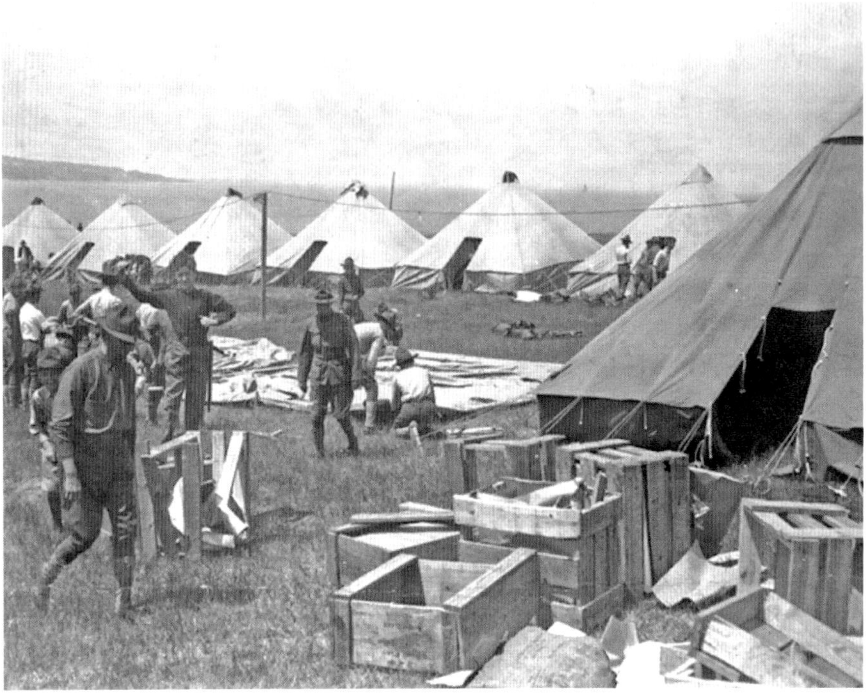

Rhode Island National Guard training at Fort Getty between World War I and World War II. *Jamestown Historical Society (P1976.024).*

of supplying the fort by water outweighed the advantages of the natural isolation. As other coastal defenses were built, Fort Greble was used only occasionally for training and was finally discontinued in 1947. The island is now a Rhode Island wildlife management area.

Fort Getty, across Dutch Harbor from Fort Greble, was the smallest of the Endicott-era forts built in Jamestown. It had three batteries. The guns of all the batteries pointed south toward the mouth of the bay. On the seaward side, the emplacements were protected by rock and dirt covered with grass.

With sixty-one and a half acres, Fort Wetherill on the East Passage was the largest of Jamestown's Endicott Fortifications. Although about 10 percent of the site had been part of old Fort Dumpling, most of the land was acquired by right of eminent domain between 1898 and 1902. The houses on the condemned properties were typically large summer homes that had been built in the 1880s. The fort was named for Captain Alexander M. Wetherill, USA, a Philadelphia-area native whose family summered in Jamestown. He was killed at the Battle of San Juan Hill on July 1, 1898.

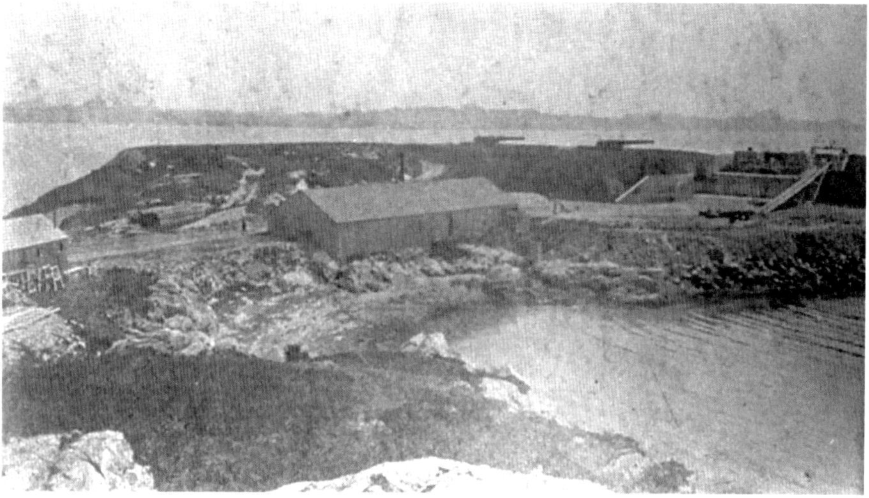

The guns of Battery Varnum (visible along the horizon). Battery Varmum was the first Fort Wetherill installation in the early twentieth century. *Jamestown Historical Society (P1982.078).*

Both Fort Getty and Fort Wetherill were garrisoned during World War I, and both were put in caretaker status between the wars. At Fort Getty, where few buildings were built before the 1930s, the ten-man barracks established in 1909 doubled as caretaker quarters during the periods of inactivity. At Fort Wetherill, the temporary barracks and support buildings built during World War I were sold to the public.

War in Europe began in September 1939. France fell on June 22, 1940. With Great Britain hard-pressed to prevent invasion, Germany had free access to the Atlantic sea lanes. In August 1940, President Franklin D. Roosevelt nationalized Rhode Island's 243rd Coast Artillery Regiment, a harbor defense regiment, and assigned it the defense of the Rhode Island coast.

Fort Getty was reactivated early in the European phase of World War II. Units of the 243rd Coast Artillery were stationed there soon after the regiment was nationalized. The guns at the fort, which were similar to those at Fort Greble, were replaced over the course of the war with more modern, mobile arms.

A massive rebuilding of Fort Wetherill began in mid-1940. Barracks to house over one thousand men were constructed, along with officers' quarters, mess halls, and other support buildings. As soon as the barracks were ready, units from the 243rd were transferred to Fort Wetherill and assumed control of batteries Crittenden, Wheaton, Varnum, and Dickenson.

Germany surrendered—ending World War II in Europe—on May 8, 1945. Soon after, the U.S. Army established a school of administration at Fort Getty and a police school at Fort Wetherill to educate anti-Nazi German prisoners of war in American democracy. Groups of 160 to 180 prisoners passed through the school every sixty days. The curriculum at the Fort Getty school included language, military government, and German and American history. The students at Fort Wetherill studied history and government with special emphasis on law and law enforcement.

When the educational activities at the forts were made public in the fall of 1945, the United States was accused of violating the Geneva Conventions and of brainwashing the POWs. The program ended abruptly in December.

The army began withdrawing from the two forts in 1946. The Town of Jamestown bought the Fort Getty property in 1955 for $5,500 with the proviso that for twenty years it would be used "for public recreation." The navy continued to use the wharf and adjacent mine complex buildings at Fort Wetherill until 1959. In 1972, the federal government declared Fort Wetherill "surplus" and, four years later, turned it over to the State of Rhode Island for a public park.

Chapter 24

Torpedo Testing from Air and Land

At the beginning of the twentieth century, Gould Island—Jamestown's third inhabitable island—was owned by a single New York family who used it as a summer retreat. The original military installation there came about as a result of the navy's research into in-water torpedoes.

The U.S. Navy established the Naval Torpedo Station on Goat Island in 1869, only eight years after the English engineer Robert Whitehead produced the world's first self-propelled torpedo. The experimental station conducted its first test firing of a propeller-driven torpedo in Narragansett Bay in 1890, and in 1908, the navy's torpedo factory on Goat Island was completed.

In early 1918, two explosions in the Goat Island facility killed some of the workers. In July, Congress authorized the president to seize Gould Island for storage of torpedoes and explosives and as a base for aircraft to test-fire aerial torpedoes.

A Naval Air Detail was established in 1920. Soon after the first torpedoes were delivered to Gould Island in 1921, two naval torpedo planes—modified by the addition of pontoons—arrived. The aircraft were used to test-drop aerial torpedoes and to track and locate torpedoes that had been test-fired from a large barge or, later, from the firing pier at the north end of the island. On November 2, 1921, Lieutenant Thomas H. Murphy, head of the Air Detail, made the first successful U.S. air drop of a torpedo in the waters off Gould Island.

The complex on Gould Island continued to grow during the late 1920s, although the actual manufacture of torpedoes dropped in response to the

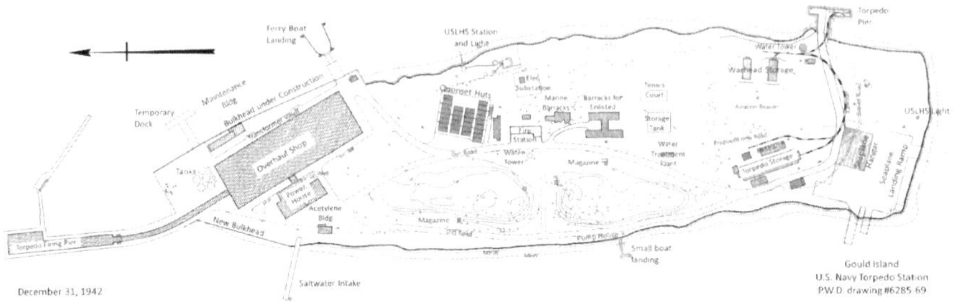

Gould Island in 1942. *Author's collection (developed from P.W.D. drawing #6285-69, public domain).*

peace initiatives of the 1920s and early 1930s. The navy announced a build-up in the mid-1930s. At the peak of World War II activity, in 1944, more than thirteen thousand men and women worked twenty-four hours a day, seven days a week, on Goat Island and produced 5,656 torpedoes in that year alone.

Three new types of torpedoes were introduced at the beginning of World War II: Mark 13 for aircraft, Mark 14 for submarines, and Mark 15 for ships. Between 1941 and 1945, 4,300 test drops of the Mark 13 were conducted near Gould Island. The Mark 14 and Mark 15 were test-fired from barges and from the Gould Island firing pier. All told, there were over 75,000 proofing tests on the Narragansett Bay ranges.

The purpose of the firings was to determine whether a torpedo's propulsion systems functioned satisfactorily and whether its guidance systems correctly controlled the torpedo's course. The torpedoes were not armed, but accidents with the test firings were not uncommon. A torpedo fired on the range in 1937 from the submarine *Cachalot* passed between two yachts, struck a ledge, leapt into the air, and ploughed through an iron fence near what is now the New York Yacht Club. In a similar incident in 1938, a torpedo fired by the test-firing barge off Gould Island came to rest near Beacon Rock, the Morgan estate on Brenton Cove. The USS *Capella* (AK-13), a government freighter, was accidentally torpedoed and damaged in 1942.

About 7 percent of the torpedoes that were fired were lost; that is, they left the range. Most of the lost torpedoes were quickly recovered, although some were still turning up many years later, especially on Prudence Island, which was at the northern end of the test range. A *Newport Daily News* story in 1960 tells of two Jamestown teenagers spotting a stray torpedo in the bay, a short distance north of the East Ferry landing.

Chapter 25

Beavertail in World War II

Between the American Revolution and World War II, most of the Beavertail peninsula was ignored by the military. Fort Getty was built at the northwestern point at the beginning of the twentieth century. During World War I, six observation posts were built on the crest of Prospect Hill just south of Fort Getty. The posts commanded a view of both the East and West Passages, and observers used sighting instruments to take bearings on targets and telephoned the data to the gun batteries at Fort Wetherill, Fort Getty, Fort Greble, and other forts around the bay. On the lower peninsula, only the lighthouse remained in federal hands.

Things changed abruptly at the beginning of World War II. Germany's fleet of submarines threatened American shipping in the Atlantic even during the European phase of the war when the United States was officially neutral. The threat to shipping and to the coast escalated after December 7, 1941. The last U-boat sunk in World War II was sunk in Rhode Island waters after it torpedoed a merchant ship off Point Judith on May 5, 1945, only days before the official German surrender.

Harbor Entrance Command Post

In October 1941, Harbor Entrance Command Posts (HECPs) were ordered at seventeen harbors in the United States to protect these strategic entry points against enemy infiltration or mining. A HECP was responsible for guiding friendly vessels safely in and out of the harbor it protected and for preventing enemy attempts to enter. Each approaching ship had to be identified. "Suspicious Vessel" procedures were initiated if questions were raised. These procedures included querying the vessel and, if the queries were not satisfactorily answered, firing warning shots from local batteries. If HECP personnel decided that the suspicious vessel was the enemy, the HECP coordinated the harbor defenses. It identified targets and assigned them to specific shore batteries. It armed and detonated the defensive mine fields.

HECP guardianship was effective across the nation. No hostile force penetrated America's harbor defenses during the war.

Beavertail was the site of the Narragansett Bay HECP. Observation of bay traffic from a hastily built shack near the lighthouse began immediately after the establishment of the post. As the operation expanded, the government acquired the land north of the light.

On December 4, 1941, four days before the declaration of war with Japan, the 185-acre Fort Burnside was established on the southern tip of the Beavertail peninsula. Fort Burnside was named for Ambrose E. Burnside, a general in the Union army during the Civil War who was later elected

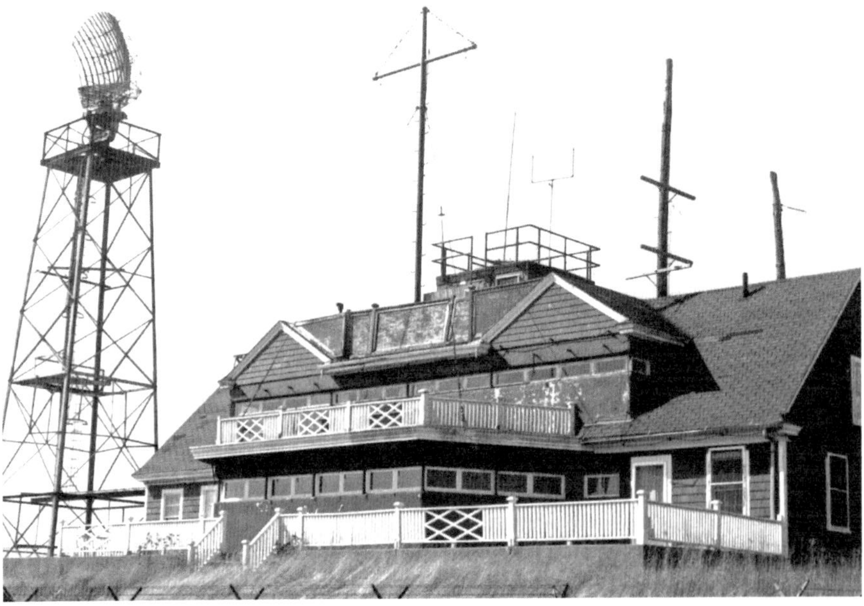

Harbor Entrance Command Post building in the 1980s. The radars were added after World War II. *Jamestown Historical Society.*

governor and then United States senator from Rhode Island. The U.S. Army fort included both the HECP and, later, the navy's radar development lab, Spraycliff.

The HECP was housed in a twenty-four-room concrete bunker, designed to look like a New England farmhouse. A series of viewing ports lined the first and second floors. Observers at the view ports used optical azimuth and range-finding instruments to calculate the position and speed of incoming vessels.

Most of the activity occurred in the basement of the HECP. A large wall map showed the coastline from Montauk Point to Cuttyhunk Island. An overlay grid showed the range arcs of coastal gun batteries in the defended area. All vessels in the area were tracked on the map.

The HECP was a joint army/navy operation. The army had general operational responsibility for the fort. The navy commanded the HECP. The army collected and correlated all information about potential targets. The navy collected underwater intelligence data in a separate area of the building, which was closed to army personnel.

A telephone system with one hundred separate lines connected the HECP in a "Hot Loop" to the Thirty-sixth Anti-Aircraft brigade and the Regional Defense Command in Boston. Both the telephone system and the backup two-way radio system were tested each shift.

The HECP was deactivated in June 1945, following Germany's surrender in May.

Spraycliff

An entirely different kind of activity was taking place in the northwestern part of Fort Burnside. Airborne radar for night fighter aircraft was crucial in the Pacific theater during World War II. Late in 1942 and into early 1943, a joint U.S. Navy/Massachusetts Institute of Technology (MIT) radar design and test complex—officially called Spraycliff, code name "Mickey"—was established north of the HECP at Fort Burnside to develop the needed technology. Five radar towers rose above a box-like field station. Fighter pilots from Naval Air Stations at Quonset and Charlestown tested and trained on the newly designed system before deploying to aircraft carriers in the Pacific.

The joint navy/MIT operation ceased in April 1945, and the installation was renamed the Naval Radio Station Newport. Two months

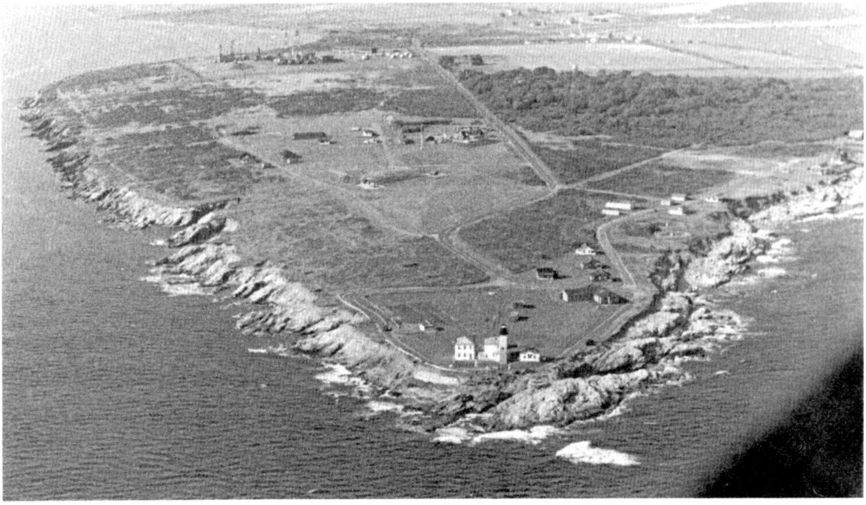

Beavertail in 1946. The Naval Radio Station (northwest section of penisula) expanded to include twenty-five radio transmission antennas. *Jamestown Historical Society (P2012.101.002).*

later, the navy incorporated the recently deactivated HECP into the communications facility.

From the beginning, Spraycliff also served as a ship and airplane Combat Information Center (CIC) training center. The training center contained the actual tactical equipment of the ship's CIC. Simulations fed target and environmental information to the replica of the CIC to train the equipment operators both in the operation of the equipment and in how to act as a team in shipboard situations.

The training operations continued after the war. In 1950, the facilities were expanded to provide fully integrated Combat Operations Center (COC) team training. Nearly every CIC/COC crew of the navy's aircraft carrier force trained at Beavertail.

Fort Burnside was transferred to the navy in 1957 and rechristened Naval Radio Station (Transmit) [US NAVRADSTA (T)]. The facility was an arm of the U.S. Naval Communications Station Newport and was functionally an expansion of the radio facility that went into operation in 1945. Twenty-five radio antennas were erected within the 185-acre complex. Each was connected to one or more of thirty transmitters. Different antennas and transmitters were used for different modes of communication. Transmission modes available included radio teletype, aircraft relay, single side-band, and Morse code to aircraft, ships, and naval bases. The Beavertail complex sent messages around the world. One unique mission assigned to the station was to serve as relay for the classified "Emergency Action Message," which could commit the nation to the use of nuclear weapons.

The naval base realignment in the early 1970s included the closure of all navy facilities in Jamestown. The Beavertail communication site officially closed in 1974, and by 1981, most of the structures had been demolished.

With the help of Rhode Island senators Claiborne Pell and John Chafee, who had been secretary of the navy from 1969 to 1972, Beavertail State Park was created from the abandoned military compound.

Chapter 26

The Retiring Navy

"It is said," reported Maud Howe Elliot in *This Was My Newport* (1944), "that if, on Conanicut Island, you closed your eyes and threw a stone you would probably hit a retired Rear Admiral." There is lots of evidence to support her statement.

Among the earliest flag officers to retire to Jamestown was Admiral David Dixon Porter (1813–1891), who rose to fame in the Civil War. With his fleet of mortar vessels—schooners armed with thirteen-inch mortars that could throw a ball weighing 241 pounds over two miles—he supported his foster brother Admiral David G. Farragut when he captured New Orleans in the spring of 1862. Porter then proceeded up the Mississippi River to use his mortar fleet at Vicksburg. After the war, he was superintendent of the U.S. Naval Academy (1865–69) and became, in 1870, only the second person to have the rank of admiral.

Like many retiring naval officers, Admiral Porter was drawn to Jamestown for its peacefulness. He once grandly told a town council meeting that although he had been in all parts of the world, Jamestown was "the healthiest and pleasantest place he had found in all his travels." He built a house at High Street and Walcott Avenue in 1888–89 but died only two years later.

During the 1880s, several active-duty naval officers made Jamestown their summer headquarters. While they were at sea or stationed abroad, their families could enjoy Jamestown. Most of them continued to spend their summers in Jamestown after their retirement.

Admiral Porter's daughter and her husband, Lieutenant (later Rear Admiral) Leavitt C. Logan (1845–1921), built their house, Meadowside, on Friendship Street at the same time and only blocks away from her father's cottage. They continued to summer there throughout their lives.

Rear Admiral Charles Henry Davis II (1845–1921, USNA 1864) built a house—since demolished—on Highland Drive. Rear Admiral Davis, the son of Rear Admiral Charles Henry Davis (1807–1877), had attended the United States Naval Academy while it was in Newport during the Civil War. He graduated just in time to see service in the war. He spent most of his career collecting and analyzing astronomical data for the Naval Observatory in Washington. When he retired in 1907, he moved to Jamestown full time and began painting. Although best known for his paintings of ships, he painted several oils of Jamestown scenes, two of which are in the Jamestown Historical Society collection.

Rear Admiral Edward Yorke McCauley (1827–1894) built Mist on Racquet Road, just east of Walcott Avenue, in 1889. Rear Admiral McCauley (other members of the family spelled the name Macauley) also came from a navy family. His great-uncle Rear Admiral Charles Stewart was an officer in active service in the U.S. Navy from 1798 to 1862. His father, Daniel Smith McCauley, started out in the navy but resigned to be appointed U.S. counsel general to Tripoli and then to Cairo.

Because of his father's appointments, the future admiral spent many of his formative years in the Near East and became a noted Egyptologist. In 1882, the American Philosophical Society published his *A Dictionary of the Egyptian Language, Containing All the Words That Have Been Defined by Egyptologists to the Present Time.* During Rear Admiral McCauley's lifetime, the walls of the living room in his Jamestown cottage were covered with paintings of the hieroglyphs he defined. A generation later, the house passed to a descendant of Rear Admiral McCauley's cousin Edward, who married Rear Admiral Herbert S. Howard (1884–1977), continuing the family's naval tradition. Rear Admiral Howard's descendants still summer at Mist.

The house directly across the street from Mist was built, also in 1889, for Lieutenant (later Rear Admiral) John Van Benthuysen Bleecker Jr. (1847–1922, USNA 1868) and his family. His father was a naval officer who had died during the Civil War, and Rear Admiral Bleecker's appointment to the Naval Academy was a result of his father's service. The family was from New York—Bleecker Street in Greenwich Village is named for his ancestors.

At the same time, just down Walcott Avenue from Bleecker's Box, as the cube-shaped house built by the Bleeckers was known, Rear Admiral

Thomas O. Selfridge Jr. (1836–1924, USNA 1854) was building his second Jamestown house, Red Top, now called Green Chimneys. He had built the Barnacle on Dumpling Drive in 1886, shortly after his three-year tour of duty as commanding officer at the Naval Torpedo Station on Goat Island in Newport.

Red Top got its name from its rooftop decorations, which were influenced by the family's interest in the Far East. Both Rear Admiral Selfridge Jr. and his father, Rear Admiral Thomas O. Selfridge Sr. (1804–1902), who visited Jamestown but never lived on the island, had served in the Far East. The father had accompanied Commodore James Biddle on the USS *Columbus* during his delivery of the first treaty between China and the United States, although he was recalled to fight in the Mexican War before the USS *Columbus*'s unsuccessful attempt to open Japan to trade with the United States.

Selfridge Jr., then a captain, was sent to Japan in 1885. His tour there did not end happily. Two years later, while he was conducting maneuvers on a supposedly uninhabited part of the Japanese coast, shells from the ship's cannons landed on a beach and did not detonate properly. They were later exploded by people from a nearby village, killing them. He was sent home and court martialed. He was exonerated, and the incident did not seem to affect his affection for the art of the Far East since Red Top was completed after the court martial. Nor did it affect his career; in 1896, he was the American naval delegate at the coronation of Russian czar Nicholas II.

By 1924, enough admirals had retired to Jamestown for the first "Admirals' Tea." That August, fourteen retired U.S. Navy and U.S. Marine Corps flag officers gathered at the home of Rear Admiral Colby M. Chester (1844–1932, USNA 1863), the only naval officer who actively served in the Civil War, the Spanish-American War, and World War I. This first tea was to commemorate the sixtieth anniversary of the Battle of Mobile Bay, an action in which Rear Admiral Colby had participated shortly after his graduation from the Naval Academy.

The oldest admiral at the party was George C. Remey (1841–1928, USNA 1859). Rear Admiral Remey had led an attempt to regain Fort Sumter in early September 1863. He was captured and spent thirteen months in a Confederate prison before being exchanged. He served as commander-in-chief of the United States naval forces in Asiatic waters during the Boxer uprising in China in 1900. For many years around the turn of the century, the Remey family summered at the Gardner House and later at the Bay View Hotel.

Rear Admiral George H. Wadleigh (1842–1927, USNA 1863), a less frequent visitor to Jamestown, was also at the party. In 1910, Rear Admiral Remey's daughter Mary had married U.S. Marine Corps lieutenant colonel John Winthrop Wadleigh, Rear Admiral Wadleigh's son. John W. Wadleigh died of yellow fever in the spring of 1923, and in 1926, Mary Remey Wadleigh built a house for herself and their two sons on Conanicus Avenue. The house was later moved to Bay View Drive. The elder son, John Remey Wadleigh (1915–1993), followed in his grandfathers' footsteps; he attended the Naval Academy and rose to the rank of rear admiral.

The youngest admiral at the 1924 gathering was Spencer S. Wood (1861–1940, USNA 1882), who had retired only three years earlier. He had commanded the battleship USS *Oklahoma* in World War I and was later in charge of the First Naval District, which included Rhode Island. Rear Admiral Wood may be the only admiral with a song written in his honor; in 1918, Chief Yeoman Daisy May Pratt Erd published the "Rear Admiral Wood One-Step."

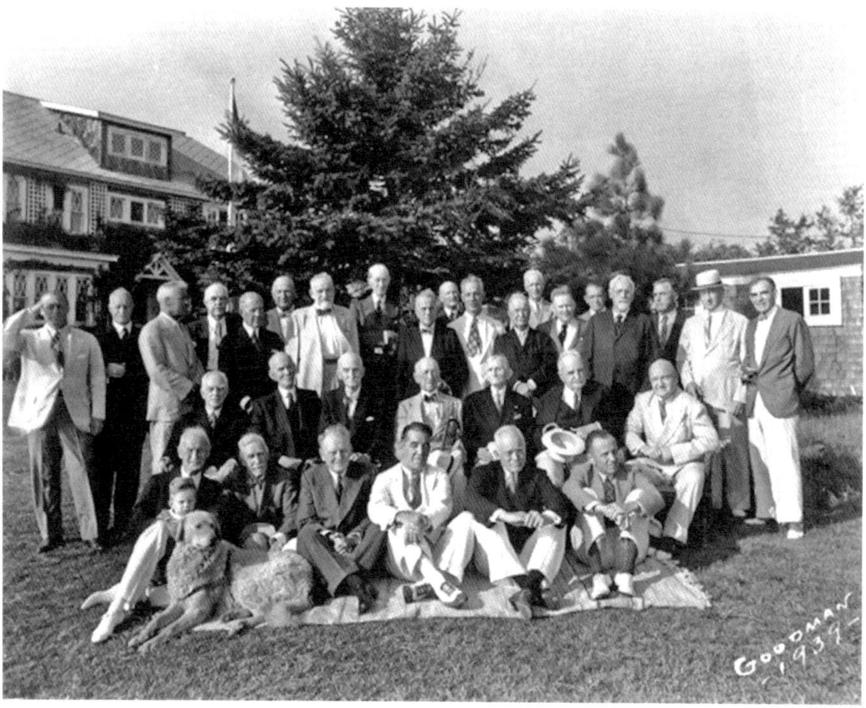

Fifteenth-annual "Admirals' Tea" in 1939. Thirty-two retired naval officers, many with homes in Jamestown, attended. *Jamestown Historical Society (P2000.021).*

Rear Admiral Wood, who built a house at West Ferry where a grandson still lives, kept the tradition of the Admirals' Tea alive until his death. A guest at his last party on August 7, 1939, counted thirty-two admirals and other navy officers.

While Rear Admiral Wood entertained the old guard, a new generation of naval officers was learning about Jamestown as they trained in Newport and sailed with the Atlantic fleet based in Narragansett Bay. For them, the transition to peaceful life in Jamestown had to wait until after World War II.

Although most of these later retirees were drawn to Jamestown by their Rhode Island experience, some already had roots on the island. Rear Admiral Alexander S. Wotherspoon (1892–1976, USNA 1915) was the son of Major General William W. Wotherspoon, the army chief of staff in 1914, who had built a house on East Shore Road in 1897. Rear Admiral Wotherspoon's specialty was ordnance, which earned him the nickname "Mr. Gun Factory." He retired to Jamestown in 1949.

Rear Admiral Edward D. Taussig (1847–1921, USNA 1867)—of the older generation—and his son Vice Admiral Joseph K. Taussig (1877–1947, USNA 1899) traced their roots to the same small part of Europe as James Taussig, who developed Shoreby Hill. Both families had settled in St. Louis, and the St. Louis connection may have attracted the naval Taussigs to Jamestown. The elder Taussig served in the Pacific during the Spanish-American War before retiring to Jamestown in 1908. Perhaps drawing on his father's Far East experience, the younger Taussig was an outspoken critic of the country's lack of preparation for war with Japan. He was reprimanded for testifying to Congress in April 1940 about the inevitably of war in the Pacific. The reprimand was rescinded on December 8, 1941, after Vice Admiral Taussig's son was badly wounded in the attack on Pearl Harbor.

Vice Admiral Taussig enjoyed Jamestown for only two years after the end of World War II, but his widow continued to summer on Shoreby Hill until her death in 1989.

The increasingly suburban character of the town after the opening of the Newport Claiborne Pell Bridge in 1969 and the relocation of Newport-based ships to southern ports in 1973 reduced the number of navy officers settling in Jamestown. But many children, grandchildren, and great-grandchildren of the earlier generations of retirees still live or summer on the island.

Part VI

Fun in the Sun

Chapter 27

The Historic Lure of Fishing

Jamestown's twenty-six miles of rocky coastline have been a lure for fishermen for centuries. Large stone-chipped spearpoints from about 3500 BCE have been found on the island. Fish were a substantial part of the islanders' diet. As late as the 1930s, the wife of the lighthouse keeper on Dutch Island complained about too much fish for dinner.

In the late nineteenth century, Jamestown began to attract large numbers of sports fishermen. Clubs and camps were established, some with extensive amenities. Among the most elaborate was the Beavertail Fishing Club, located several hundred yards northeast of the lighthouse. According to reports in the *Newport Journal* in the 1893–94 off-season, the club's new building would have "a dining room on the first floor and sleeping rooms above for the use of the employees of the club" with a twenty- by forty-foot stable nearby.

Robert Goelet was from a very wealthy New York real estate family. He had a mansion on Fifth Avenue and an oceanfront estate in Newport, but for fishing, he came to Jamestown. His "camp" on Beavertail differed very little from a Jamestown summer cottage, and he entertained there lavishly. Two reports in the Newport papers in 1907 tell of the ferry *Conanicut* making special after-hours trips to carry his guests back to Newport after parties.

Peckham's Camp was both less elaborate and more commercial. A promotional brochure from the turn of the century advertised "seven bungalows fitted only for camp life, three of which are let for a term of years. The rental price is $100 for the season of four months."

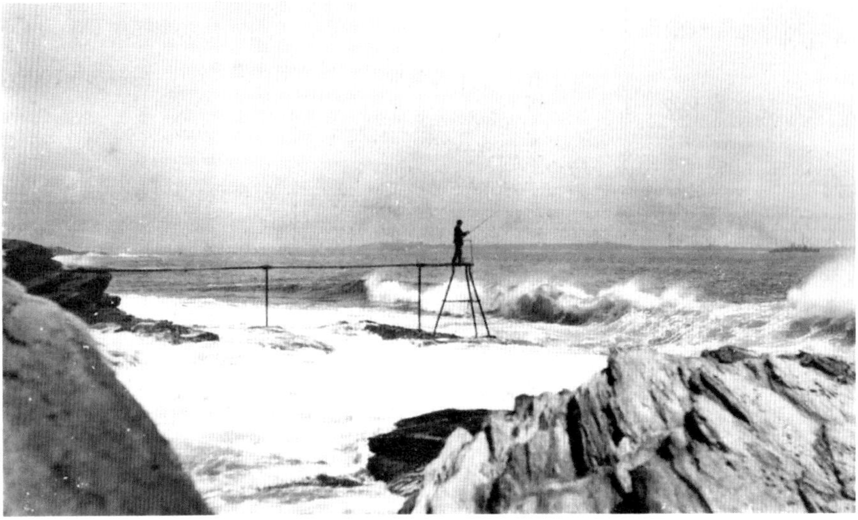

A single-person fishing stand at Beavertail. The stands brought fishermen out over deeper water in search of striped bass. *Jamestown Historical Society (P2012.029.019).*

The main activity of all these clubs was fishing. To give members and guests a better opportunity for a successful catch, fish stands were built. These iron-supported platforms extended from the top of a rocky bank straight out over the roaring surf. The narrow walkway allowed one person at a time to reach the end of the stand and cast his line farther out into the bay.

Most fishermen made their catches from the rocky shoreline. The most popular rocks were identified by name. Beavertail Fishing Club anglers could fish from Lucky Strike, Rip Rap, Old Slippery, or Yellow Dirt. Farther north were rocks named Spindle, Lion's Head, Flat Rock, and the Pulpit.

The opportunity to access a favored rock had to be tempered with an awareness of the perils associated with these slippery surfaces. Accidents, some of them fatal, were reported periodically. One tragedy that closely affected Jamestown occurred in mid-October 1932. As the *Newport Daily News* reported, "Ernest Vieira had gone fishing off the rocks at Horsehead with three companions. A storm-driven wave struck and swept all four into the water." Ernest Vieira, Manuel Medeiros, and Joseph Mello Sr. were drowned. Joseph Mello Jr., the son of Joseph Sr., was the sole survivor. All four men were Jamestowners. Ernest Vieira left behind a pregnant wife, two teenage sons and a younger daughter, and a thriving delivery service business.

The species that enter the bay in the twenty-first century are the same species from earlier times. The quantity and the size of the fish caught differ dramatically. "Mr. John E. Watson and Mr. William Gardner captured more than a hundred pounds of blackfish (tautog) Wednesday," reported the *Newport Journal* on October 5, 1889. "Thousands of blackfish [were] caught from the rocks" during late October 1895, according to the *Journal*. The largest blackfish caught with rod, reel, and line in the 1924 season, again according to the *Journal*, weighed eleven and three-quarter pounds and was twenty-six and a half inches long with a girth of twenty-three inches.

Striped bass were less abundant, and it was size rather than numbers that counted. A forty-pound bass caught with rod and reel from one of the fishing stands made the news in August 1883. The largest striped bass taken from Jamestown's shores was landed in October 1936. Jamestowner Arthur S. Clarke caught the sixty-five-pound striper at Hull's Cove.

Bluefish were of little interest to the sports fishermen, although when they were running they were quite plentiful. Cod, which at the beginning of the twentieth century could be caught in the bay off Beavertail in large numbers and occasionally landed from the rocks, was of much greater interest. "A 60

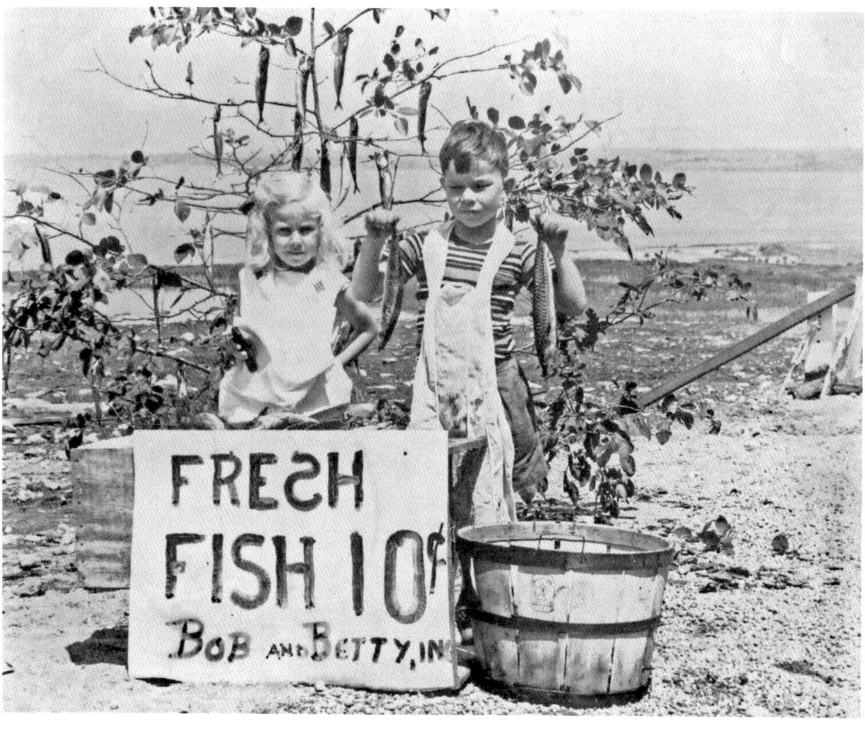

"Bob [Clarke] and Betty [Lyons], Inc." selling freshly caught fish at East Ferry in 1940. *Jamestown Historical Society (P2001.102).*

pound codfish was caught Wednesday with hook and line in the west bay by Mr. Andrew King," reported the *Newport Journal* on January 12, 1907. The Kings were bay pilots who lived near West Ferry.

During and for a while after World War II, Beavertail was closed to the public. However, by the early 1950s, it once again became a destination point, although access was restricted except during the summer months. The fishing piers and clubhouses were gone, and fishing contests and derbies were sponsored by fishing clubs, business associations, and bait shops with the express purpose of attracting sportsmen to local waters.

The first contest of note was sponsored by the Jamestown Businessmen's Association in 1948. The *Newport Daily News* reported that the largest bass, caught by Harry Locke, weighed eighteen and three-quarter pounds and the largest black fish, caught by John Peters, weighed seven and a quarter pounds. The following year, the Jamestown Rod and Gun Club sponsored a striped bass and surf fishing contest, and the Newport Chamber of Commerce and a group of Jamestown businessmen also conducted a fishing derby. The Jamestown Businessmen's Association continued sponsoring fishing contests through the mid-1970s. They also instituted the fishing derby at the Jamestown reservoir for youngsters five to fourteen years old that is now an annual event of the Jamestown Striper Club.

At the same time that Beavertail was being put off limits by the military, a new opportunity opened for fishermen seeking bay access that improved their chances of success. After the Jamestown Bridge was built in 1940, fishermen walked out on the bridge sidewalk to get to deeper waters that might hold larger striped bass or bluefish. As automobile traffic increased, this practice became controversial. Motorists complained of lures and lead

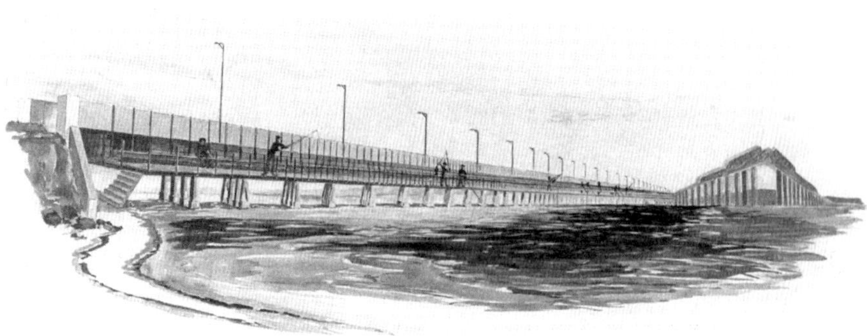

Proposed catwalk to be dedicated to fishing from the old Jamestown Bridge. *Jamestown Historical Society (P1984.128).*

sinkers flying close to their windshields and of fish and debris lying on the walkway next to the fishermen.

Early in March 1974, state officials announced plans to construct a one-thousand-foot-long platform or catwalk on the North Kingstown end of the bridge. However, just in case these plans fell through, in April of that same year, four separate bills to ban fishing from the bridge were introduced in the legislature. The platform was never built, and the issue finally went away when the new Jamestown Verrazzano Bridge opened in 1992 with no pedestrian access at all.

Jamestown is still a popular place to fish. A 2015 article in the online magazine *Surfcasting Rhode Island* explained why: "For the surf angler, Beavertail affords a distinct advantage seldom encountered—The ability to hit deep water and retrieve across multiple drop-offs."

Chapter 28

Animals and Islands

Jamestown dogs seem to have a particular affinity for ferries.

In 1892, Captain I.B. Briggs owned a water spaniel named Toby. Each morning, Toby took the early ferryboat to Newport to get his owner's morning paper. He would leave his home at about 6:00 a.m. and trot a mile to the ferry. He usually made the trip across the East Passage with the captain in the pilothouse on the upper deck. Arriving in Newport, he picked up the morning paper and sometimes a friend would place a bit of meat in a paper bag for the dog's breakfast. He then returned to the ferry with the newspaper. If all went well, his master received the paper shortly after 10:00 a.m.

Seventy years later, in the early 1960s, two basset hounds commuted regularly on the same route. The two dogs—the older one named Lord Dempsey and the younger Gibson—were unrelated, but both seemed to have caught the traveling bug.

Lord Dempsey started his excursions to Newport as a puppy in 1961. He started out with brief trips, taking the 7:00 a.m. ferryboat to Newport and returning to Jamestown on the same ferry. His owner, Mrs. Jon Adamowicz, tried to break Dempsey's traveling habit by taking him for a walk at 6:00 a.m. every morning in a direction away from the East Ferry wharf. "I got tired of getting up at 5:30 a.m.," she explained later, "and stopped taking him for supervised walks." Lord Dempsey returned to his interrupted travels on a new schedule. He became a regular passenger on the 8:30 a.m. ferry to Newport and punctually returned home on the 2:30 p.m. boat.

On the Newport side, he normally spent the morning either cavorting with fellow canines on Pelham Street or resting. Two of his favorite resting spots were the police station on Market Square and a liquor store on Broadway. Sometimes he would return to bury a bone near the ferry landing.

The sad-eyed hound curtailed his excursions after he was hit by a car. When his convalescence was over, the lure of his girlfriends occasionally drew him back to Newport aboard the ferryboat, and they would romp for old time's sake.

While Lord Dempsey gracefully waddled into his declining years, another hot-blooded basset entered his prime and carried on the traveling tradition. Gibson was two years old in 1967 when Captain and Mrs. Theodore Waterbury of Shoreby Hill rescued him from the Potter Animal Shelter in Newport and brought him to Jamestown. A navy couple had left Gibson at the shelter when they were transferred to Washington, D.C., so he was quite familiar with Newport and evidently longed for his old haunts.

Gibson kept a less rigid schedule than his predecessor and sometimes went on weeklong benders. His trips to Newport took him to bars and parties. The social dog crashed a party at the Newport Yacht Club, and during the America's Cup races, he was found at the Ida Lewis Yacht Club. One of his favorite spots was the Black Pearl on West Pelham Street. Since he was quite a rogue among the female canines, Gibson was sterilized. That attempt to end his rambling ways was unsuccessful, and he continued to make excursions to Newport until the ferries were discontinued in 1969.

When some of your people are in Jamestown and some are in Newport, the reason to travel is even more compelling. Sammy was one Jamestown dog in that situation. One of his owners worked for the Jamestown & Newport Ferry Company in Newport. The family lived in Jamestown, and another family member worked at the Jamestown Recreation Center, right across from the East Ferry landing. When Sammy was told, "Mommy is in Newport. Go find her," he would trot across the lines of traffic waiting for the next ferry. The deckhands would let him on without question. He would then join his mistress in the ferry company's Newport office and come home with her at the end of the day.

Sandy, a cocker spaniel, faced a more complex dilemma. Iona and William Dailey owned the Harbor View Nursing Home on Conanicus Avenue between the Bay View Hotel and the entrance to Shoreby Hill. Their daughter Margaret and grandson Ron lived in Newport. Sandy took the ferry back and forth between his two homes. Unfortunately, in the mid-1950s, non-paying passengers were frowned upon, but in February 1959, the

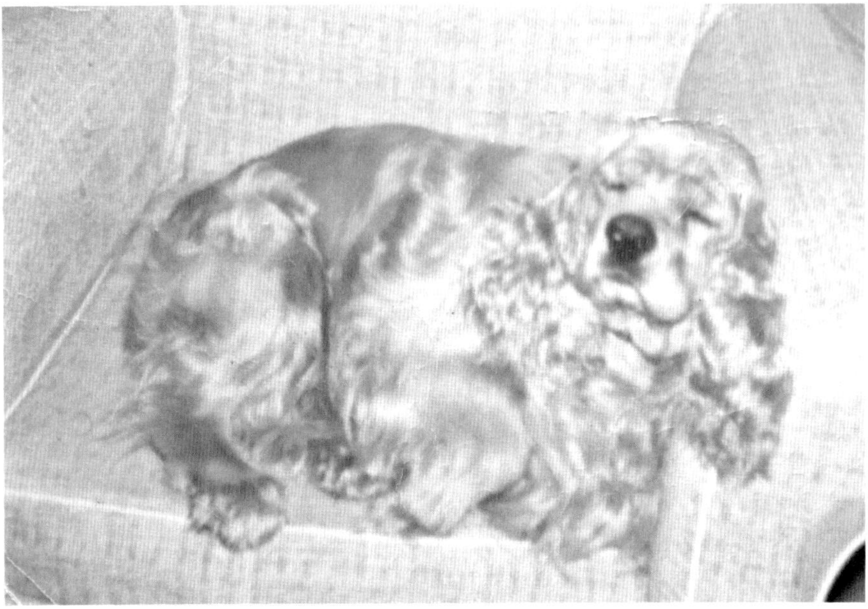

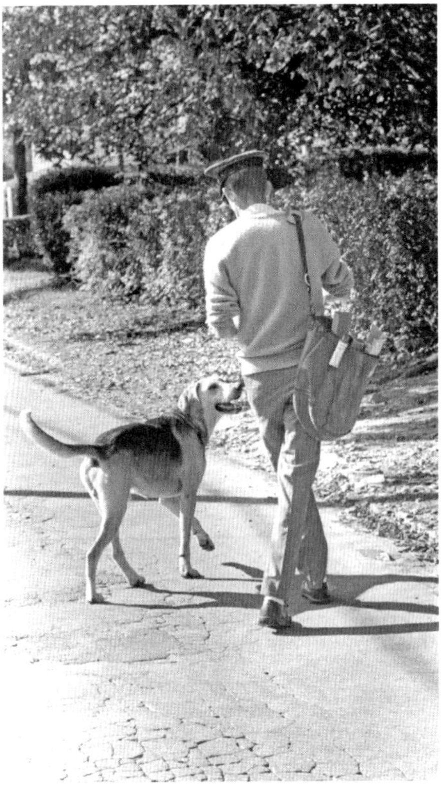

Above: Sandy, one of the dogs that hitchhiked on the Jamestown-Newport ferry. *Courtesy of Carol Hopkins.*

Left: Tramp, the "postman." Every day, Tramp joined letter carrier Bill "Mac" McCarthy on his daily rounds. *Jamestown Historical Society (P1984.016).*

Public Works director who controlled the ferry decided that the dog could have a free pass. About the same time, the family was reunited in Jamestown, so Sandy didn't need his pass after all.

Other Jamestown dogs kept their wandering to more local scenes in the days before the leash laws.

"Staff Sergeant" Murphy was a mixed-breed mutt that trained with the 243rd Coast Artillery at Fort Wetherill before World War II. He wore staff sergeant stripes and even went on "liberty" in Newport. When Murphy died after being hit by a truck, he was given a hero's funeral and was buried next to the flagpole at the fort. His memorial stone, now in the Artillery Grounds next to the Jamestown Historical Society museum, reads "St. Sgt. Murphy, Canine Mascot. Hq. Bty. 243d. CA. Died Feb. 11, 1941 Game to the Last." His stone, like the stones of other veterans in the cemetery, is marked with an American flag each Memorial and Veterans Day.

Tramp lived on Grinnell Street, but in the 1970s, he met Bill "Mac" McCarthy every day at the Jamestown Post Office and accompanied him on his daily rounds.

Chapter 29

A Yacht Club for Jamestown

In the late nineteenth and early twentieth centuries, summer visitors to Jamestown often settled in for the whole summer. They founded private clubs and built clubhouses at which to meet and socialize. The only remaining private club from the era is the Conanicut Yacht Club.

Yachting became a popular pastime on Narragansett Bay in the late nineteenth century. The Rhode Island Yacht Club was incorporated in 1877, and the Zephyr Boat Club, which morphed into the Bristol Yacht Club, began the same year. In the summer of 1891, a group of Jamestown summer residents—most of them from the Philadelphia area—met to discuss a yacht club for Jamestown, and in October 1892, the State of Rhode Island issued a Certificate of Incorporation to the Conanicut Yacht Club.

The following spring, a covered pier was erected on land purchased by the club on the east side of Conanicus Avenue at the end of Brook Street. (At the time, the road along the shore—now called Conanicus Avenue—ended at Brook Street. To go farther south, one turned west on Brook and then south on what is now Old Walcott but was then simply Walcott Avenue.) The first clubhouse, built partially over the water on pilings, opened in 1894. A general clubroom, committee room, photographic darkroom, and similar amenities occupied the first floor. The second floor was devoted to a "ladies room"—that is, a lounge and changing room for women only—surrounded by a wide porch. By 1900, 122 member families paid annual dues of five dollars each.

The roster of members of the Conanicut Yacht Club also listed most of the members in the Jamestown Club, a men's-only social club, and in

1916, as the First World War began to affect the social life of Jamestown, the "Jimtown Club," as it was called, merged with the yacht club. The yacht club immediately built a new and larger clubhouse, designed by Philadelphian Herbert Wetherill, who also designed the Jamestown fire station. The new clubhouse extended farther out over the pier and provided more rooms for socializing for both men and women.

The merged club devoted itself to enjoyment—mostly, but not exclusively, enjoyment of Narragansett Bay. Many of the older members owned fully staffed motor or sailing yachts, ranging in size from *Wild Duck*, a 143-foot power yacht owned by Charles B. and Madge Levey, to much smaller catboats and sloops. The younger set raced in the club's fleet of pilots, dories and triangles.

The club sponsored an annual "Watersports"—a day-long marathon of marine-related competitions open to all town residents. Diving contestants would dive from two diving boards or from the roof of the pavilion at the end of the long yacht club pier. Swimmers swam laps between a float out in the bay and the float at the pier. Young people in canoes jousted with

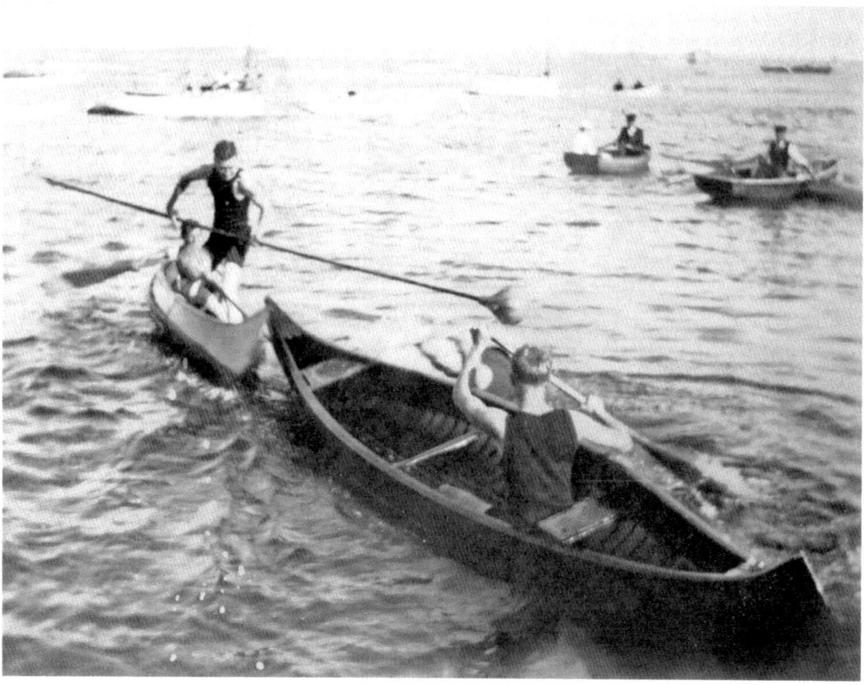

Canoe jousting, one of the popular sports at the Conanicut Yacht Club annual "Watersports." *Jamestown Historical Society (P2013.115.041).*

"lances" made of greased and padded masts. And, of course, boat races for all classes—or no class at all—were held. According to club records, "townies" triumphed in most of the events.

The dance floors in the new clubhouse saw dancing through the night. The club hosted weekly dances. In June 1918, the club steward returned after closing the club for the evening to find a large party in progress—hosted by a woman who wasn't even a member of the club. Other times the unauthorized use of the hall was only discovered the next morning when the debris of the previous evening had to be cleaned up.

Despite the social nature of the club, rule number six in 1900 read: "No liquors of any description can be used on Club property, nor on board of any boat made fast to wharf or floats." The passing of the eighteenth amendment

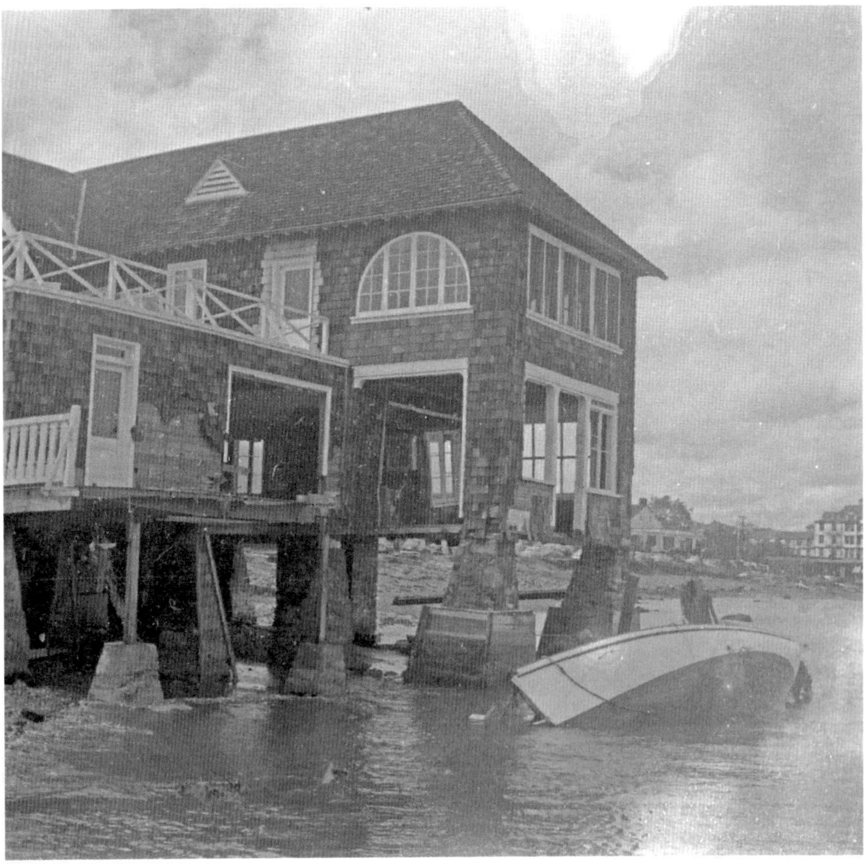

The old Conanicut Yacht Club pier and building after Hurricane Carol, 1954. *Jamestown Historical Society, Umstead Collection (P2014.110.043).*

to the U.S. Constitution and the Volstead Act to enforce prohibition in 1919 made the rule moot, but even after the twenty-first amendment repealed Prohibition in 1933, bar facilities remained private. The "5:00 Club" met almost daily for happy hour, and men in the reading room had access to stock in a private cupboard. The first club bar was established in 1948.

Other changes came in the post–World War II years. The population of Jamestown was growing quickly. Many new residents, with many interests, wanted to join the club. Tennis was added to the club's sports inventory in 1951 with the leasing and later acquisition of the Jamestown Golf and Country Club tennis courts on Shoreby Hill. Canasta and bridge parties took the place of earlier whist parties. Races and cruises—and, of course, dining and dancing—continued.

The Hurricane of 1938 had wiped out the yacht club pier, but—based on the amount spent for repairs, only $1,850—left the twenty-year-old clubhouse relatively unscathed. Hurricane Carol in 1954 was a different story. The yacht club's entire fleet was lost, the pier was destroyed, and wave after wave crashed through the clubhouse. A year of controversy followed. Should the almost forty-year-old clubhouse be rebuilt or restored, or should the club move to a new location?

In 1955, the club settled into the 1890s Shingle-style cottage on Bay View Drive from which it still organizes social and sporting events for its members. Over the years, the club has expanded the building to include an enclosed porch, a larger lounge area, and other facilities.

Chapter 30

Golf Courses and Golf Clubs

Golf became popular in the United States about the same time that Jamestown became a fashionable summer resort. The country's first golf clubs—and because of the cost of setting up and maintaining a golf course, golf almost always involved a committed membership that paid the basic expenses—were organized in the late 1880s.

Jamestown had more than its share of golf enthusiasts, especially among the summer visitors. The first golf course, the nine-hole Conanicut Golf Club, was started in 1895 at Blueberry Lane and Walcott Avenue. An organizational meeting for the Conanicut Golf Club was held on July 6, 1895, at the cottage of Dr. O.F. Wadsworth. The twelve founding members elected Dr. Wadsworth chairman of the meeting and then the club's first president. R.G. Wadsworth was elected secretary and treasurer, and Captain J.R. Green, Charles Wharton, Dr. George McClellan, and Miss Mary Macauley were named to an executive committee.

Bylaws were adopted. Membership was limited to twenty-five members. Two weeks later, at the next recorded meeting, the bylaws were amended to allow for thirty-six members and up to fifteen one-year associate memberships. A week later, another amendment changed the active membership to fifty.

Only residents of Jamestown—"a member of a family that owns a cottage or has hired one for the season"—were eligible. Entrance fee was two dollars, with an annual assessment to be fixed by the executive committee from year to year. Members whose assessment was in arrears more than two months would be dropped from the club by the executive committee. No strangers could play on the course unless accompanied by a member, but invitations might be extended to guests of members and approved by the executive committee.

The club leased land on the Cottrell property and laid out the course with holes along Walcott Avenue, Stanton Road, and Highland Drive. The land was really still farmland. One of the rules of play in the handwritten rule book reads, "Manure may be moved at all times." The hazards on the course included stone walls and hay stacks. The treasurer's records show payment on October 3, 1904, to Alton Head of fifteen dollars for "keeping up bull." The ladies of the club were having a tournament that day and did not wish to contend with an untethered bull roaming the fairways.

On September 2, 1897, the *Newport Daily News* reported that golf had become very popular with the Jamestown people, and that many visited the links at the Dumplings every pleasant day.

Roads turned out to be the major hazards on the new courses. At the beginning of the 1900 season, the *Newport Journal* reported, "Owing to the danger and inconvenience caused last season by the frequent crossings on the links of the Conanicut Golf Club, the number of holes has been changed from nine to six and all crossing has been avoided."

Condition of the farmland course continued to be a concern. The same article contained a tepid endorsement: "While the fair green is not by any means perfect, it is seldom one gets an unplayable lie. The putting greens have improved from year to year and are moderately true." A month later, however, a report on the golf tournament was less positive: "Considering the grounds upon which the game was played the scores were good."

The Conanicut Golf Club existed for only the brief period from 1895 to 1903—just nine summers. Each year, a full complement of fifty regular members and, after 1898, fifty associate members signed up. Names on the roster remained pretty much the same each year, with an occasional new one appearing. The list included many familiar summer families: Wetherill, Green, Wharton, Hopkins, Crawford, Warden, McClellan, Hazard, Lippincott, Pemberton, Sedgwick. Retired military were represented as well with Rear Admiral T.O. Selfridge, Captain and Mrs. J.R. Green, and Colonel and Mrs. F.V. Greene. A goodly number of single ladies were members—the Misses Mary and Ellen Macauley, Gertrude M. Rice, Carolyn Newhall, Edith Richmond, Isabel Wetherill, Elsie Bleecker, and one listed simply as Miss Barringer.

Financially, the club was a success. Each new season began with a balance on hand. The major costs were $12.00 a year to rent the land from A.H.

Peckham and a monthly payment to Alton Head for taking care of the course. Head's charges moved slowing upward from $30.00 to $40.00 and then to $50.00. Still, the 1900 season started with a carryover balance of $100.23.

While the maximum number of members stayed the same, annual assessment fees for both members and associate members were increased to three dollars in 1903.

The final written minutes of the club are dated July 4, 1903. Miss Elizabeth Clark hosted the meeting. Six members of the board were present. Rear Admiral Selfridge presided. The treasurer reported previous year receipts of

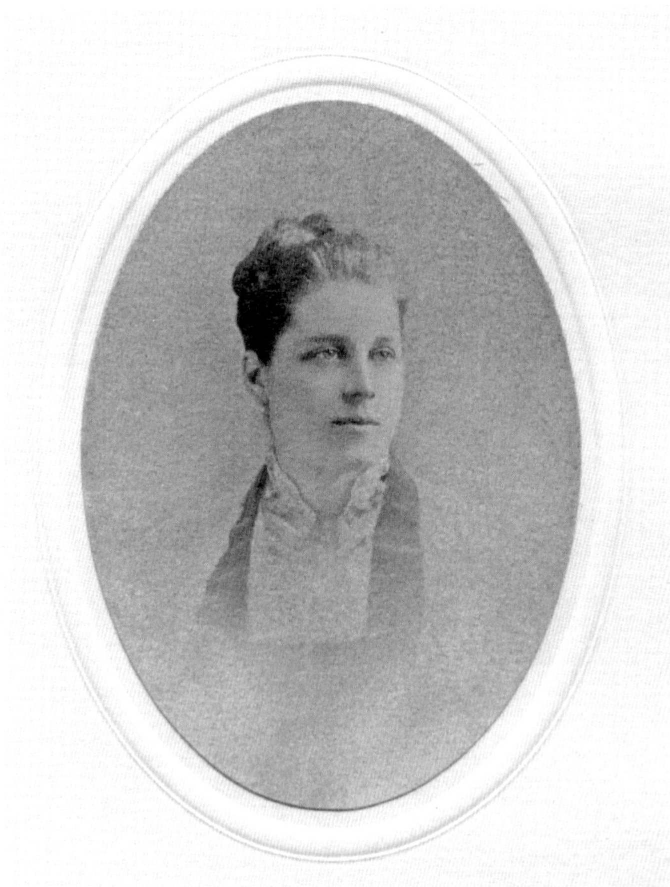

Miss Elizabeth Clark, secretary for zoologist Alexander Agassiz. She hosted the last recorded meeting of the Conanicut Golf Club board. *Jamestown Historical Society (P2012.114.002).*

$168.73 and expenditures of $80.43 leaving a balance of $80.42 to start the new season.

Only a treasurer's report exists for the year 1904—sixteen members had paid their assessment. Nothing is recorded for 1905, and a brief financial report dated July 1906 showed that $79.71, plus $8.04 interest, remained in the club treasury. Nothing more.

The demise of the Conanicut Golf Club coincided with the rise of a new golfing venue. Talk of organizing another club began as early as 1899 when issues with the road hazards became evident. In 1901, the Jamestown Golf and Country Club turned talk into reality.

The new course was laid out on the leased Littlefield farm north of the village. The "clubhouse" was two rooms in the Littlefield farmhouse. The founders were five summer residents. Dr. David Bell Birney, a Philadelphia physician, had an active summer practice on Union Street in Jamestown. Albert Lawrence Wetherill was one of a large number of Wetherills who summered on the island and a cousin of Alexander Macomb Wetherill for whom Fort Wetherill is named. Thomas Chester Wallbridge, a banker from Germantown, Pennsylvania; John L. Davis, a Shoreby Hill resident from St. Louis; and Henry H. Luther, a Newport dentist and son of one of Jamestown's first realtors, completed the group. The officers of the new club lived in or near the village, so the course was definitely more convenient for them.

The club officially opened on August 3, 1901. According to the *Newport Journal*, the event was celebrated with a tea and reception. Cottagers and hotel guests chatted and strolled on the lawn and listened to the music of Howard's Orchestra. An open golf match for ladies and gentlemen was played on a temporary nine-hole course. The following year, Alexander H. Findlay, one the earliest acknowledged golf course architects, designed the permanent course.

A committee was formed at the end of the summer to determine what to do to give the club members more space. Should the club take over the entire farmhouse or would it be better to have a building designed to the club member's needs?

A new structure was decided on, and Andrews and Withers, a Newport architectural firm, was hired to design it. The one-story building was fifty feet by twenty-seven and a half feet. A twelve-foot wide veranda, roofed by extensions of the building's gables, circled the structure on three sides, making its actual footprint about seventy-four feet by forty feet. Inside were men's and ladies' locker rooms, dressing rooms and showers and a good-sized pantry.

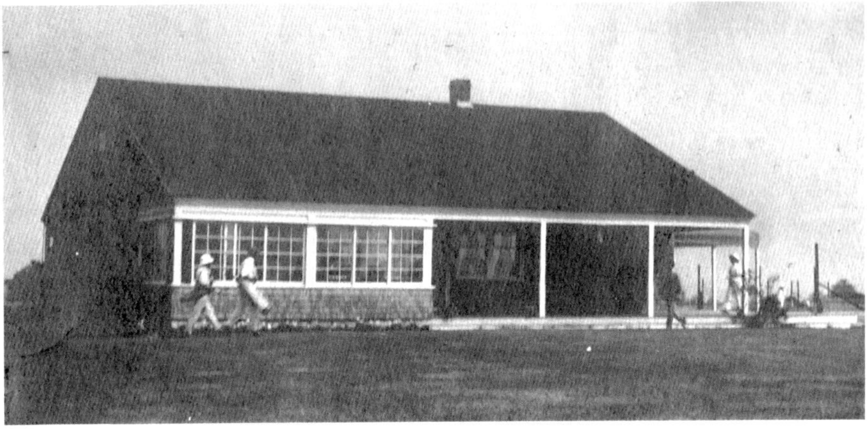

The Jamestown Golf and Country Club building about 1912. A matching veranda on the side facing the golf course was unenclosed. *Jamestown Historical Society (P1985W.216).*

The building was constructed on the south side of the golf course, at Standish and Whittier Roads, by Louis Wayland Anthony, a Jamestown builder and architect who was active on the island well into the 1930s. The Andrews and Withers design blended well with the Shoreby Hill homes around it.

The clubhouse served not just the golfers but also those who used the tennis courts (which now belong to the Conanicut Yacht Club) the bowling green to the south of the building, and the croquet lawn. A Porch Membership was also available—for three dollars, one could enjoy the clubhouse porches, without participating in any of the sports offered.

During the first fifty years, the clubhouse saw few changes. Almost immediately after the building was completed, the veranda on the side of the building that faced Whittier Road was glassed in, and ping-pong and pool tables were installed. Everything else remained the same. Then, in 1946, Frederick H. Clarke, who had acquired the Littlefield farm through a mortgage default, sold the property to the Lyons family. The Lyonses in turn sold the tennis courts to the Conanicut Yacht Club and moved the clubhouse to Conanicus Avenue in 1951.

Two years after the clubhouse was moved, Francis and Lily Costa bought it along with the seventy-five-acre course. They upgraded the course and, over the years, made significant changes to the aging building. The verandas were enclosed. An addition on the north created a 130-seat restaurant, and part of the original building was converted to a 100-seat bar and lounge. Kitchen and storage facilities were added on the west side.

When the Costas decided to sell the course in 1986, the town bought it—paying for the purchase in part by selling the development rights, thus ensuring that the land would remain open space.

The Jamestown Golf and Country Club is the only remaining golf course in Jamestown. But for sixteen years from 1926 to 1942, a second course prospered on the island. The eighteen-hole Beavertail Golf Club course was designed by A.W. Tillinghast, who also redesigned the Newport Country Club course in 1923. Nine of the holes were on the Mackerel Cove side of Beavertail Road, and nine overlooked the West Passage.

By all reports, it was a beautiful and challenging course. The names given to the holes indicate their beauty and their hazards: Parapet, Cliffs, Douglas, Sentinel, Stone House, Brook Hall, Piggley (where pigs once were kept), Twin Rocks, Farm House, Landing Brook, Pebbley Beach, Pinnacle, Wall, Long Meadow, Harbor View, Bayberry, Tilly's Rest (named for Tillinghast), and Dublin Road.

Chapter 31

Camp Seaside

Rhode Island's Young Women's Christian Association, now simply the YWCA, was incorporated in January 1870, only fifteen years after the movement to address the needs of young working women took root in England. Its initial mission was to provide a comfortable Christian home for women whose earnings were small and who were often without family in the city where they worked.

In the summer of 1877, the organization faced a new problem. A young woman in its Providence house was ill, and the doctor advised her to go to the seashore.

Jamestown was the ideal place. The island had a reputation for being especially healthful. In 1881, the *Newport Daily News*, quoting statistics from the State Board of Health, reported that "the rate of mortality [in Jamestown] is less than in any other town in the state." Its sea breezes brought comfort in the summer heat, and its beauties included peaceful pastures and panoramic views of Narragansett Bay.

The association found an ideal house. At what would now be 864 East Shore Road stood the Oliver Hopkins farmhouse. No date of construction is available, but it was probably built sometime in the eighteenth century, since it is described as "old" in 1881. The farmhouse was owned by John and Laurana D. Kendrick, who had joined with Lucius C. Davis in the development of Conanicut Park, and it stood near the southern edge of the plat. The area was easily reached from Providence by the steamer that landed a few blocks north at Broad Street. The Kendricks offered the YWCA

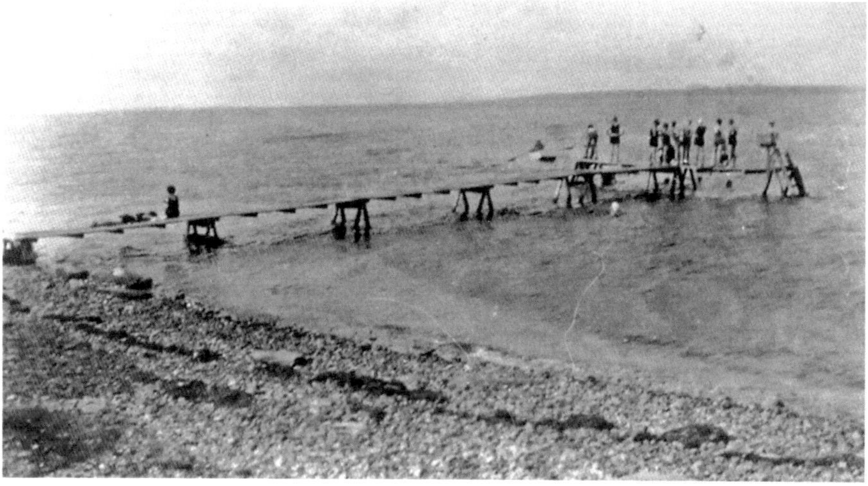

Camp Seaside wharf, 1929. The message on the back of this postcard reads, "Camp wharf from which all swimming lessons were taken as well as Life Saving classes." *Jamestown Historical Society (P1994.004).*

the use of the house, free of charge. The farmhouse was christened Seaside Cottage and became the nucleus of a camp for workingwomen needing an outing for change and rest.

The house was quickly furnished with a variety of donated pieces. An appeal in the *Providence Journal* generated sufficient funds to begin housekeeping. Most of the labor to put the house in order and oversee the summer activities was donated. As the *Journal* reported in 1881, "someone always being found ready and willing to perform this labor of love."

Seaside Cottage was not large, and only nine or ten women could live there at any one time. Each boarder paid three dollars a week for which they received a bed, healthy food three times a day, and the leisure to swim, play tennis, wander around the North End, or just do nothing. Stays were limited to two weeks, with exceptions allowed in special cases. In the first year, 29 boarders and 118 day visitors, most of them in poor health, stayed at the camp.

For three years, the number of women staying at the camp increased—forty-seven in the second year and sixty-five in the third—but the facility did not. In the spring and early summer of 1881, with the camp's finances in the black, the YWCA bought Seaside Cottage and the surrounding land from the Kendricks and adjacent lots from Thomas Carr Watson, reserving in each transaction "the so-called Hopkins burying ground and the passage thereto." (The burial ground no longer exists and is not listed as a historic Rhode Island cemetery.) The total recorded cost was $2,010. With the property secured, the Sea Side Home, as it was then called, closed on Saturday, September 3, to expand and repair the facility.

Later that year, Elizabeth E. Andrews, one of the camp's strongest supporters, paid the Conanicut Land Company ten dollars and "other valuable considerations" for the right to use the well on the property next to Seaside Cottage. A year and a half later, she sold her rights to the YWCA for ten dollars.

Mothers and their children had been welcomed at Seaside Cottage only for two weeks in late August. In 1881, the Kendrick cottage, next door to Seaside Cottage, was purchased so that city children and their mothers could come throughout the summer. A festival was held at the Conanicut Park Hotel to help pay for the cottage. The *Newport Journal* reported the event in detail.

> *The day proved pleasant and agreeable. A brisk breeze came up the bay, affording comfort to all concerned in the good work. Two large tents were pitched in front of the hotel, and the summer houses were gaily decorated with flags and bunting. The flag staff of the yacht club bore a multitude of nautical insignia, and several of the cottages were arrayed with flags, etc., in harmony with the occasion.*
>
> *The first boat from Providence brought a large company, including Bishop Clark and other prominent citizens, who are interested in the enterprise. A goodly company also came from Newport, so that the hotel and grounds soon presented a lively appearance...At 4:00 P.M., quite an addition was made on the arrival of the second boat from Providence and an hour or so later there was still another arrival of visitors from Newport, some five hundred in all participating in the exercises.*

The event netted $700.

The camp continued to grow and prosper for twenty years. One of the most delightful descriptions of those years is found in Mariana M. Tallman's *Pleasant Places in Rhode Island*, published by the Providence Journal Co. in 1893.

> *But the most notable and most praiseworthy feature of* [Conanicut Park] *is the institution known as Seaside Cottage, the admirable arrangement by which tired, ill or not over-wealthy city women and children may have a week or two of change and absolute rest at the small sum of $3 per week. Mrs. Wright, the matron, has charge for the fourth season, and her domain is a most delightful one. Picture a quaint, low, old-fashioned grey farmhouse, with deep well and flat door stones, enlarged by ell and verandahs, and nestled*

> *in the heart of a quiet old apple orchard, with huge gnarled trunks, where the sun and shade frolic in the breezes that blow up the salt waves, lapping the rocks almost at its foot. In a hollowed stone by the old well, the birds drink and bathe in a tiny pool, and twitter perpetually. This is* Seaside Cottage, *and a winding concrete walk leads down to the "children's cottage," under the same jurisdiction, but where mothers with little folk abide, that the nervous and invalid be not disturbed at the larger house—a thoughtful provision which we would commend to the attention of hotel keepers generally. Mrs. White is assistant matron here. There are times when the matron has been called upon to entertain ninety in her entire fold…*
>
> *Mrs. Wright showed us the mammoth great range recently acquired, with mingled pride and despondency; for though an indispensable, it is not yet paid for. Our errand was hailed with joy, for the matron assured us that the place was seldom "written up" without some kind response in the form of a much-needed check; and hopes were high that a similar demonstration might follow our coming, and settle the range difficulty, and the still more vexed water question; for the old well, though mightily picturesque, is not practical, and Mrs. Wright lamented in almost Scriptural phrasing that her five handmaidens had nothing wherewith to draw, and the well was deep…Of the good that is done the matron speaks in unstinted measure. "The girl clerks and telegraph operators who come here are dead tired—out and out," she says: "They have no appetite, no strength, no color at first, and it does my heart good to see them improve as they breathe the fresh air, and walk, and bathe, or just do nothing."*

The era of cooperation between the Seaside cottages and the summer residents of Conanicut Park could not go on. In July 1900, 260 women and children were living in the expanded facility. In September 1901, the YWCA decided to erect a large dormitory, 182 feet long by 80 feet wide and three stories high, just north of the cottage. This was too much for the Conanicut Park Improvement Society. The organization drafted a letter to the YWCA pointing out that the grounds and shore facilities were inadequate for the number of boarders admitted at present and to increase the size of the buildings to accommodate a greater number would still further overcrowd the grounds and cause a still greater encroachment upon the property and rights of others. In addition, the letter pointed out crowding always tends to bring about unsanitary conditions, especially in those days when the raw sewage was pumped directly into the bay. The group also requested that the character of boarders be more properly guarded, a reference to incidents of trespassing and vandalism.

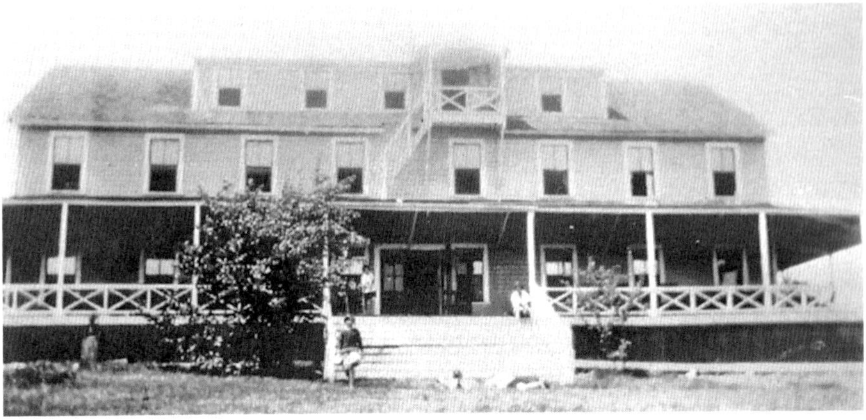

Nunksqua Cottage, a dormitory at Camp Seaside, was built after the 1904 fire that destroyed a camp building. *Jamestown Historical Society (P1994.005).*

The dormitory was built anyway. How much the resulting strained relations affected the next major event at Camp Seaside is a matter of conjecture.

On April 9, 1904, a grass fire broke out near the Camp Seaside cottages. According to the story in the *Newport Journal*, no assistance was requested for a half hour until "it was feared that the S.M. Vose cottage, situated about 50 feet to the south, would catch." This despite the fact that, according to the *Journal* report, there were only six men available in Conanicut Park to fight the fire. (The Vose cottage, Cajacet, was not part of the Conanicut Park plat.)

The Jamestown fire department volunteers left for Conanicut Park at 11:30 a.m., although even then doubts were expressed about whether the apparatus should go, "as there were some who remembered an ordinance providing that the department should not attend fires beyond the north bridge."

It took the Jamestown volunteers almost an hour and a half to drag their equipment up the wretched roads between the town and Conanicut Park. Once there, they "practically saved the Park from being wiped out," to quote the *Journal* report.

The "children's cottage" was totally destroyed, and several other buildings were damaged. The YWCA rebuilt the complex over the next few years.

As the Conanicut Park development slowly declined, the friction between the two constituencies also declined. The YWCA mission to provide a place for workingwomen to rest lessened, too, as working conditions, if not wages, improved. By the 1940s, Camp Seaside, which operated until 1970, was indistinguishable from any other girls' summer camp.

Selected Bibliography

Armbrust, Henry N. Method for Cleaning a Submerged Surface, US Patent #3,226,259, issued December 28, 1965. (Jamestown Historical Society Collection, A2006.117.001).

Buttrick, James C. "Charles Lovatt Bevins, Jamestown's English Architect." *Newport History, Journal of the Newport Historical Society* 78, no. 260 (Spring 2009): 36–63.

Buttrick, James C., with the Jamestown Historical Society. *Images of America: Jamestown.* Charleston, SC: Arcadia Publishing, 2003.

Carr, Edson Irving. *The Carr Family Records, Embacing [*sic*] the Record of the First Families who Settled in America and their Descendants, with Many Branches Who Came to This Country at a Later Date.* Rockton, IL: Herald Printing House, 1894. http://books.google.com/books.

Chadwick, Mrs. French E. "The Visit of General Washington to Newport in 1781." *Special Bulletin of the Newport Historical Society*, February 1913.

Champlin, Richard. "Lore of Conanicut Island's Springs." *Jamestown Press*, October 7, 1993.

Cogar, William B. *Dictionary of Admirals of the U.S. Navy, Volume 1: 1862–1900.* Annapolis, MD: Naval Institute Press, 1989.

Enright, Rosemary. "Defending Our Shores: Military Installations in Jamestown." Exhibit program, Jamestown Historical Society, 2015.

Enright, Rosemary, and Sue Maden. "Allowing People into Town, Kicking People Out." *Jamestown Press*, April 12, 2012.

———. "Daniel Watson: Early Development of Real Estate in Jamestown." *Jamestown Press*, May 31, 2013.

———. "From Operator to Dial Tone." *Jamestown Press*, October 9, 2014.

———. "General Washington Marches Down Narragansett Avenue." *Jamestown Press*, April 11, 2013.

———. "An Island Clubhouse." *Jamestown Press*, November 28, 2013.

———. *Jamestown: A History of Narragansett Bay's Island Town*. Charleston, SC: The History Press, 2010.

———. "Jamestown's First Summer Community." *Jamestown Press*, August 23, 2012.

———. "Jamestown Shores: Building a Community of Summer Cottages." *Jamestown Press*, January 4, 2013.

———. "Joseph Clarke and Descendants Make Lasting Contribution." *Jamestown Press*, August 15, 2013.

———. "The Poor You Will Always Have with You." *Jamestown Press*, June 28, 2012.

———. "The Retiring Navy." *Jamestown Press*, October 25, 2012.

———. "Shoreby Hill: An Exceptional Garden Suburb." *Jamestown Press*, September 20, 2012.

———. "Summer Cottages for Rent." *Jamestown Press*, September 6, 2013.

———. "Torpedo Manufacturing on Goat and Gould Islands." *Jamestown Press*, February 28 and March 28, 2013.

———. "A Yacht Club in Jamestown." *Jamestown Press*, July 3, 2013.

Historic and Architectural Resources of Jamestown, Rhode Island. Providence, RI: Rhode Island Historical Preservation & Heritage Commission, 1995.

Jamestown Historical Society. "An Agreement of Several of the Free Inhabitants," (1657 Pre-purchase contract for Conanicut and Dutch Islands). A2006.461.001.

———. "Conanicut Golf Club—Secretary." A2008.300.022.

———. "Conanicut Golf Club—Treasurer." A2008.300.023.

———. "Jeanette S. Sharrer House at Plat 8, lot 19." A2006.466.001.

———. "Remembrance of the History of the Jamestown Shores Association," (Compiled for the celebration of fifty years of incorporation as a neighborhood association, June 25, 2000). A2013.602.001.

Karentz, Varoujan. *Beavertail Light Station on Conanicut Island: Its Use, Development and History from 1749*. Charleston, SC: Book Surge Publishing, 2008.

———. "Beavertail. World War II 1942–1945. Spraycliff (Mickey) Site and 1946–1974 US Navy Communications Station." Research paper. Photocopy, 2012.

———. "Harbor Entrance Command Post at Fort Burnside." Research paper. Photocopy, 2000.

Knowles, William G. 1872. Improvement in Washing-Machines, US Patent # 126,463, issued May 7, 1872. (Jamestown Historical Society Collection, A2006.116.001).

Maden, Sue. *Greetings from Jamestown, Rhode Island: Picture Post Card Views 1900–1950.* Jamestown, RI: West Ferry Press, 1988.

———. *The Jamestown Bridge, 1940–2007: Concept to Demolition.* Jamestown, RI: Jamestown Press, 2007.

Maden, Sue, with images by Dick Allphin and Tom McCandless. *The Building Boom in Jamestown, Rhode Island, 1926–1931: Buildings, Builders, People Associated with the Buildings, a Glimpse of Life in this Era.* Jamestown, RI: West Ferry Press, 2004.

Maden, Suc, and Helen Richardson. "Bringing Lights to Jamestown." *Jamestown Press*, August 5, 2004, and August 19, 2004.

———. "Jamestown's Camp Seaside, 1877 to 1970." *Jamestown Press*, April 1, 2004.

———. "Jamestown's Movable Chapel." *Jamestown Press*, November 13, 2003, and November 20, 2003.

———. "The Rise and Fall of Conanicut Park, 1872–1909." *Jamestown Press*, May 17, 2001; July 12, 2001; July 26, 2001; August 9, 2001; March 28, 2002; and May 9, 2002.

———. "Water, Water Everywhere." *Jamestown Press*, August 20, 1998, and August 27, 1997.

Maden, Sue, and Janet Cooper, compilers. *The Electric Spark: A Monthly Chronicle of Jamestown Happenings. Issued by the Dr. Bates Sanitarium, 1910–1935.* Jamestown, RI: West Ferry Press, 1996.

Maden, Sue, and Joyce Allphin. "The Jamestown Golf and Country Club: 1901–2001." *Jamestown Press*, August 2, 2001.

Maden, Sue, and Nancy Keith. "Jamestown's Direct Steamship Service Between New York and Fall River on the Enterprise Line." *Jamestown Press*, July 10, 1997.

Maden, Sue, and Patrick Hodgkin. "The Birth of Shoreby Hill. A 'Residential Suburb.'" *Jamestown Press*, February 20, 1997.

———. "The First Portable House in Jamestown." *Jamestown Press*, March 28, 1997.

———. *Jamestown Affairs: A Miscellany of Historical Flashbacks.* Jamestown, RI: West Ferry Press, 1996.

———. "Number Please?!! The Telephone in Jamestown." *Jamestown Press*, June 12, 1997.

Maden, Sue, and Rosemary Enright. "The Dr. Bates Sanitarium in Jamestown, 1900–1944." *Newport History, Journal of the Newport Historical Society* 78, no. 260 (Spring 2009): 1–35.

Maden, Sue, and Tom McCandless. "The Historic Lure of Fishing Conanicut Island." *Jamestown Press*, August 4, 2005.

Miner, Mary R. "Clingstone." Jamestown Historical Society newsletter (1984).

———. "The House Near Conanicut Spring." Jamestown Historical Society newsletter (Spring 1994).

Perkins, Paul J. "Beavertail Stones and the Wrecked Schooner *H.F. Payton*." Privately printed, 2003.

Preston, Reverend Charles E. *The First Movable Church: The Chapel of the Transfiguration, Conanicut Island*. Privately printed, 1899.

Schroder, Walter K. *Defenses of Narragansett Bay in World War II*. Providence: Rhode Island Bicentennial Foundation, 1980.

———. *Images of America: Dutch Island and Fort Greble*. Dover, NH: Arcadia Publishing, 1998.

Watson, W.L. *History of Jamestown on Conanicut Island in the State of Rhode Island*. Providence, RI: John F. Greene Co., Inc., 1949.

———. *The House of Carr. A Historical Sketch of the Carr Family from 1450 to 1926*. Program for Carr family reunion. Privately printed, 1926.

Weeden, Louise Mary. "A Few Items of Interest to the Weeden Family." Handwritten. Jamestown Historical Society Collection, A.2014.123.003. c. 1893.

"Winners of 'Bridge Memories' announced." *Jamestown Press*, April 6, 2006.

Wood, Virginia Steele. "A Rhode Island Patriot in Newport Jail: The Diary of Benjamin Underwood of Jamestown." *Journal of Newport History* 71, part 1 (2000).

LOCAL NEWPAPERS

Jamestown (RI) Electric Spark
Jamestown (RI) Press
Newport (RI) Daily News
Newport (RI) Journal
Newport (RI) Mercury
Providence (RI) Journal
Wickford (RI) Standard Times

ONLINE DATABASES

Ancestry. http://www.ancestry.com.
Newspapers. http://www.newspapers.com.
http://books.google.com/books.
United States Patent and Copyright Office. http://patft.uspto.gov.

INTERVIEWS

Emeline Cabral, August 2015.
Arthur C. Clarke III, August and September 2015.
Elizabeth Di Censo, August 2015.
Mary Greene, August 2015.
Judy Hannold, July and August 2015.
Carol Hopkins, April and August 2015.
Mary Beth Murphy, August 2013.

Index

C

D

Y

About the Authors

Sue Maden grew up in Cleveland, Ohio, and she has master's degrees in both public health nursing and library science. Before moving to Jamestown, she worked as a librarian at Columbia University in New York City.

Sue's family has been coming to Jamestown in the summer since the 1880s. She and her husband, Phil, moved to the island permanently in 1982 and built a house next to the old family home overlooking the West Passage. She immediately immersed herself in Jamestown history, and in 1988, she published her first book on the subject, *Greetings from*

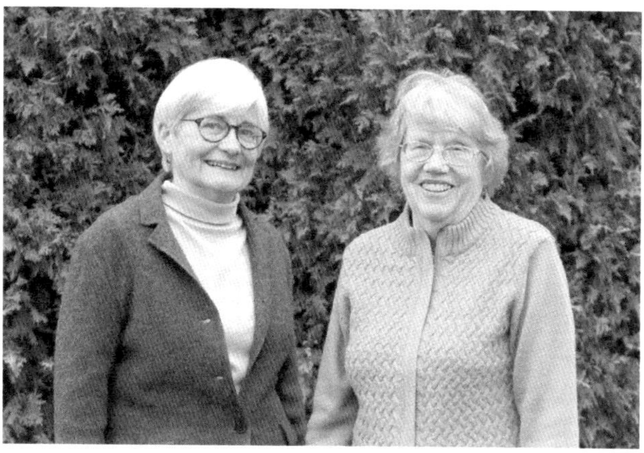

Authors Rosemary Enright (left) and Sue Maden. *Photograph by Jeff McDonough.*

Jamestown, Rhode Island: Picture Post Card Views 1900–1950. Since then, she has written over one hundred articles, columns, and books about local history.

Sue is an active member of the Jamestown Historical Society, devoting practically full time to her volunteer activities there. She served on the society's board for eighteen years and is currently the society's archivist. She is also a member of the Publications Committee of the Newport Historical Society.

Rosemary Enright grew up in Buffalo, New York, and did graduate work in American studies at New York University in New York City. She moved to Jamestown in 1974 with her husband, Bill Slattery. Bill's forbearers had—like Sue's—summered in Jamestown for one hundred years. The stories he told about life on the island in his childhood sparked her interest in the town's history.

In 2003, she volunteered to take over the editing of the Jamestown Historical Society's newsletter. Since then, she has continued writing about local history and about the society for the local press. She has also designed and created exhibits that show off the holdings of the society. She has served on the board of the society for twelve years and is currently president.

Until 2007, Rosemary worked for Northrup Grumman Corporation as a project manager and process engineer. She is a member of the Jamestown Town Planning Commission and of the board of the Jamestown Community Piano Association.